ACTS of prayer

An imaginative approach to spending time with God

Susan McDonough
and Mandy Welburn

kevin mayhew

First published in Great Britain in 2008 by Kevin Mayhew Ltd
Buxhall, Stowmarket, Suffolk IP14 3BW
Tel: +44 (0) 1449 737978 Fax: +44 (0) 1449 737834
E-mail: info@kevinmayhewltd.com

www.kevinmayhew.com

9 8 7 6 5 4 3 2 1 0

ISBN 978 1 84867 034 1
Catalogue No. 1501108

Cover design by Rob Mortonson
Edited by Rebecca Vaughan-Williams
Typeset by Fiona Connell-Finch

Printed and bound in Great Britain

Contents

Foreword

Prayer is the life-breath of every Christian. Without it we die within. Yet there are times when we feel exhausted, run-down, or just plain low energy. At such times we need some help – an oxygen mask, or someone to tell us to breathe more slowly, more deeply, or in a more focused way.

Susan McDonough and Mandy Welburn have developed just that help. This unique aid plunders a wide treasury of meditations, scripture passages, songs and hymns, and brings them together in a way which will invigorate and never bore. This is because they have created a fascinating way of uniting any combination of Adoration – Confession – Thanksgiving – Supplication (A. C. T. S.).

It can be used as a springboard for private prayer or for leading worship in public liturgy. It is thoroughly grounded in a desire to develop our relationship with God, and I commend it wholeheartedly.

Martin Wallace

† Bishop of Selby

Acknowledgements

This book has been made possible by the support of many people who have encouraged us over the three years that it has taken from conception to publication. We would like to thank our husbands, Terence and Eric, who never doubted us. We are grateful to our friends Jean, Tim and Kirsty who agreed to use the draft copy over a period of time and to give feedback, enabling us to improve on our original idea. Special thanks go to the Archbishop of York, John Sentamu, and to the Bishop of Selby, Martin Wallace, for their enthusiasm for the book and for their willingness to endorse it.

Bible Version Abbreviations

CEV	Contemporary English Version
ESV	English Standard Version
JB	Jerusalem Bible
KJV	King James Version
NEB	New English Bible
NIRV	New International Reader's Version
NIV	New International Version
NIV(UK)	New International Version (UK)
NJB	New Jerusalem Bible
NKJV	New King James Version
NLT	New Living Translation
NLV	New Life Version
NRSV	New Revised Standard Version
RSV	Revised Standard Version
TM	The Message
TYB	The Youth Bible
WWE(NT)	Worldwide English (New Testament)

In Christ Alone

In Christ alone my hope is found,
he is my light, my strength, my song;
this cornerstone, this solid ground,
firm through the fiercest drought and storm.
What heights of love, what depths of peace,
when fears are stilled, when strivings cease!
My comforter, my all in all,
here in the love of Christ I stand.

In Christ alone! – who took on flesh,
fullness of God in helpless babe!
This gift of love and righteousness,
scorned by the ones he came to save:
till on that cross as Jesus died,
the wrath of God was satisfied –
for every sin on him was laid;
here in the death of Christ I live.

There in the ground his body lay,
light of the world by darkness slain:
then bursting forth in glorious day
up from the grave he rose again!
And as he stands in victory
sin's curse has lost its grip on me,
for I am his and he is mine –
bought with the precious blood
of Christ.

No guilt in life, no fear in death,
this is the power of Christ in me;
from life's first cry to final breath,
Jesus commands my destiny.
No power of hell, no scheme of man,
can ever pluck me from his hand;
till he returns or calls me home,
here in the power of Christ I'll stand!

Stuart Townend and Keith Getty

Part One
INTRODUCTION

How It All Started

At our local church, many of us are involved in homegroups and have spent time at various points over the years focusing on our prayer lives. Having already reached the point where we knew the importance of prayer, what we needed now were ideas that we hoped might enrich our individual walk with God. However, the one problem we all had in common was our struggle to find practical and effective ways to enrich our prayers. Suggestions like post-it notes on the fridge door, music, prayer areas and candles, whilst inspiring, were not enough. We needed guidance.

A structured guide was considered helpful yet somewhat limiting in that, over time, it often reduced prayer to a routine. After debating the problem over many weeks, it was agreed that a structured approach that offered variety would stimulate and encourage us to spring forward in our prayerful journey. Unfortunately, variety equates with quantity, and not all of us can afford the time or the money to collect a wealth of materials to maintain such variety. What was needed was a resource that could offer variety for prayer within a single medium. This was as far as our final meeting on the subject took the group, but we were left with lingering thoughts that nudged us firmly towards the challenge of providing such a resource.

Our response to this challenge is a prayer book with a difference. It is a book of carefully chosen pieces designed as springboards to launch you into your own prayers. This is not a book of prayers in its own right; if it is used with this expectation it will not make sense. You need to take the written words, mull over them and absorb their message. By doing this, we hope that you will be stimulated and encouraged to offer your own prayers within the themes of the structured sections of A.C.T.S.

Why A.C.T.S.?

A.C.T.S. is an acronym that has been used by Christians worldwide for many years. It is a format for prayer in four parts: Adoration, Confession, Thanksgiving and Supplication. We chose this format because we feel that once we understand why we pray in the way that we do, and when we are provided with the means to do so, our spiritual journey will be refreshed. Many of us in our homegroups were already familiar with A.C.T.S. and had found the concept easy to understand and use. Better still, it offered a way to balance our prayers so that our communication with God was focused more on him and less on ourselves.

The effectiveness of A.C.T.S. however, was limited by our lack of creativity, our ignorance and our inability to express ourselves properly. Instead of nurturing a spontaneous and enriched prayer life, A.C.T.S. on its own had very often led to some stultified and repetitive monologues. A.C.T.S. with variety, however, was considered an encouraging and uplifting resource that not only inspired us to worship more meaningfully, but also motivated us to read our Bibles more often and with more purpose.

A Closer Look at A.C.T.S.

In order to use the format effectively, it is important to understand the meaning of each of the four aspects of prayer as suggested in A.C.T.S. They are not positioned randomly to make a neat and snappy acronym; nor are they to be regarded as separate prayer activities to be used as a blanket of devotion. On the contrary, each section is specifically linked so that our communication with God is worshipful, humble, appreciative and thoughtful. This is the mindset that we want to develop, and so counteract the tendency and temptation for prayer to be mainly petition.

Adoration

Adoration opens our prayer time by focusing on God and offering him our worship. Understanding the supremacy of God inspires us to humility and paves the way for our:

Confession

We can admit to our sins because we are assured that we are in the presence of a loving and forgiving God. Such love and security demands our:

Thanksgiving

for who he is, for his love for us and for the world. Reminding ourselves of all our blessings, and thanking God for them, leads us on to finish our prayer time with:

Supplication

which is important to God and now in its proper place.

Each of these aspects is looked at in more detail over the next few pages. We hope that you will read through them before embarking on the book itself, as they are written to help you get the best from the prayers.

Adoration

Creation's anthem will rise to you.
All the universe is crying out for you
in adoration to the Holy One,
in higher praises to the awesome God.

Clothed with Splendour Andy Bromley and Chris Donohue

Take time to reflect on this chorus; think especially about the word 'awesome'. Its traditional meaning of 'amazed adoration' has been diluted by usage, implying enthusiastic approval on a par with 'cool' and 'brill'. While God is indeed 'cool' and 'brill', he is also breathtaking, overwhelming, splendid and fearsome; in other words, he is awesome. We are in awe of him.

But is it the same kind of 'awesome' that causes crowds of adoring fans to jostle for the chance to see even a glimpse of their chosen celebrity? Some may have walked for miles or camped out overnight just to be sure of buying that precious ticket. The thrill of seeing or even meeting an idol can be inspiring; every detail, every moment is savoured, committed to memory and shared with others long after the event. Something about these celebrities makes us behave like this. Usually these 'heroes' display characteristics we admire – skills in leadership, a particular sport, a musical instrument, acting . . . By being in their presence, we are uplifted and sometimes even encouraged to emulate them. How often have we seen an increased number of people playing tennis in June! Yet at the same time, we are reminded of our own limitations and how much we fail to match even their level of skill.

And what of the celebrities themselves? Would they be interested in us and, if so, why? For one thing, having a fan base means that they are recognised and respected in their field. That must make them feel good about themselves. It boosts their egos. They love to hear other people's praise. It motivates them to work towards achieving even greater and more daring things. Not only this, but their livelihoods depend on us: no fans, no income. They need us to survive. So is this what it is like with God? Is he some self-serving persona looking for praise to buffer his personality? Does he want us to worship him merely to boost his ego? Is it a fix for him? Does he need us? No. After all, he is complete.

'"I am the Alpha and the Omega," says the Lord God, who is, who was, and who is to come, the Almighty.'

Revelation 1:8 NJB

God does not need us in order for him to survive. He will not pale into insignificance if we ignore him, nor cease to exist if we do not adore him. He is awesome, the great 'I Am' (Exodus 3:14). This is why our adoration should be God-centred; we worship him not 'in order to *feel* wonderful, we do it because God is wonderful'. (Archbishop Sentamu)

Nevertheless, God does long for us to be in his presence. He enjoys our company and wants us to enjoy his. He wants us to be as excited and thrilled about spending time with him, as he is with us. He wants us to savour every moment spent in his presence and for us to leave feeling uplifted and renewed and wanting to share our experience with others. God wants us to desire to come back again and again to be with him.

'As a deer yearns for running streams, so I
yearn for you, my God.
I thirst for God, the living God; when shall
I go to see the face of God?'

Psalm 42:1,2 NJB

But why does God long so much for us? Unlike our celebrity heroes, he wants us simply because he loves us. He knows that by spending time in his presence we will get to know him better and experience the depth of his love. After all, God is love and out of love flow the awesome qualities that inspire us to worship him. By dwelling on his nature, is it little wonder that we should want to adore him? Who would not want to be in the presence of a God like this and offer him adoration and worship? He is not a celebrity because he has achieved 'good' things; he is the almighty and creator God, perfect in personality and worthy of our worship and praise.

'Praise the Lord.
How good it is to sing praises to our God,
how pleasant and fitting to praise him!'

Psalm 147:1 NIV

Confession

How deep the Father's love for us,
how vast beyond all measure,
that he should give his only Son
to make a wretch his treasure.

How Deep the Father's Love Stuart Townend

As we spend time in God's loving presence and become more aware of him and his perfect nature, it is inevitable that we will begin to see ourselves for what we really are. Our eyes are opened to the reality of our failings and consequently to our sinfulness. God sees this reality but looks deeper to the potential of our renewal so that our sinfulness does not remain an impenetrable barrier.

All sin is ultimately behaviour against God and if we want to progress in our relationship with him we need to address this. We need to be clean in his presence and cleared of all the clutter that stands in the way of serving him effectively. Confession is the means of achieving this.

So what is confession?

The New Bible Dictionary describes confession as an outward (verbal) sign of repentance (a change of mind). It is interesting to note that the Old and New Testament writers did not look at the mind, spirit and body as separate parts of a person. Indeed, they were interlinked – each one affecting the others. Therefore, any change of mind (repentance) implied a change in attitude and therefore a change in behaviour (Proverbs 28:13; Matthew 3:8). It is not just throwing up our hands when we have been found out and saying, 'Yes, it was me!' We have no need for this kind of admission; after all, God already knows. Rather it means saying, 'Yes, I did it, I'm sorry and I resolve not to do it again.' Repentance is turning back to God (Zechariah 1:3,4). David knew how important it was when he promoted the act of confessing 'sins to the Lord' (Psalm 32:1-5). He knew from experience the results that heartfelt confession brings when a relationship with God is restored (Psalm 51:12). Confession then is a combination of admitting that we have done wrong, being sorry and being determined to change.

To be honest

Honesty with God about ourselves is crucial at this point.

'If we say we have no sin, we deceive ourselves, and the truth is not in us. If we confess our sins, he who is faithful and just, will forgive our sins and cleanse us from all unrighteousness.'

1 John 1:8,9 NRSV

If we cannot be truthful with God, then everything in our relationship with him becomes superficial. If at first glance this statement seems harsh, that is because it is. Honesty is painful. But, just as David found confession to be spiritually purifying, so too can we feel the wonderful benefits. The writer of Proverbs was also convinced of this when he wrote that our spirits would indeed prosper (Proverbs 28:13). We belong to a God who wants us to grow and flourish and to enjoy a loving relationship with him. Confessing our sins ensures that God will listen to us (Psalm 66:18,19) and will respond as a loving, merciful and just Father.

All this might seem rather daunting at first; and rightly so, because when we take a good, clear look at ourselves we find it difficult to imagine that God would ever want to fix his eyes on us, let alone have a loving relationship with us. When someone has wronged us it takes a huge effort on our part to forgive and even if we succeed, we might not forget. But God is a God whose love is 'vast, beyond all measure'. He offers us his grace, 'giving us things we do not deserve and shielding us from things we do deserve' (Alister McGrath, *Beyond the Quiet Time)*. We may be overwhelmed by our failings but they must never be allowed to affect that sure confidence we have in knowing that, through his great sacrifice of love in Jesus, we can approach God freely and safely and receive his grace.

'Let us then approach the throne of grace with confidence, so that we may receive mercy and find grace to help us in our time of need.'

Hebrews 4:16 NIV

Thanksgiving

I am a new creation,
no more in condemnation,
here in the grace of God I stand.
My heart is overflowing,
my love just keeps on growing,
here in the grace of God I stand.

I Am a New Creation Dave Bilbrough

The feeling of unworthiness that confession brings needs to be balanced with the realisation that we are welcomed into God's presence; forgiven, clothed in pure garments, white as snow (Isaiah 1:18; Hebrews 10:22). Able now, by God's grace, to approach his eternal throne and delight in his presence, our hearts are uplifted. A sense of thankfulness wells up. The book of Psalms is full of exhortations to thankfulness. It is not hard to see why; God has given us, as a people, many blessings. The grace to sit in his presence, the good news of his love for us, the gift of the Holy Spirit as our comforter and guide, and the great sacrifice of Jesus as an atonement for our sins (1 John 2:2) all inspire awesome gratitude. It is not surprising, therefore, that at this point in our devotions we feel moved to thank God, not just as our Creator but as our Saviour and Lord.

'And once again I look upon the cross
  where you died,
I'm humbled by your mercy and I'm
  broken inside.
Once again I thank you,
once again I pour out my life.'

Once Again Matt Redman

The wonderful sense of gratitude at his favour towards us opens the floodgates of thankfulness for the many personal blessings that God has bestowed on us. If at the start of the prayer session we thought that we had little to be thankful for, it is time to think again! To appreciate just some of the many blessings that deserve our heartfelt thanks, contemplate his word, the Bible, family and friends (1 Corinthians 1:4), problems overcome (1 Thessalonians 1:3,4) and prayers answered (Philippians 1:19). As St Paul encourages us in his letters, both by example and command, we should be offering thanks to God for all things at all times.

'Sing and make music in your heart to the Lord, always giving thanks to God the Father for everything, in the name of our Lord Jesus Christ.'

Ephesians 5:19b, 20 NIV

What is our response then to a God who warmly invites us into his presence and graciously forgives us? Of course it is initially thanks; thanks for his grace and overwhelming love for us. But more importantly it is because of this love, because of its openness, that we find ourselves wanting to act in response, by resubmitting ourselves to our heavenly Father.

'Yet what I can I give him – give my heart.'

In the Bleak Mid-winter Christina Rossetti

Supplication

Restore, O Lord,
the honour of your name,
in works of sovereign power
come shake the earth again;
that all may see,
and come with reverent fear
to the living God,
whose kingdom shall outlast the years.

Restore, O Lord Graham Kendrick and Chris Rolinson

The Greek word for supplication is 'deesis', which means 'a petition or a request'. Petition is bringing our needs or, as in the case of intercession, the needs of others, before God. Our prayers of supplication are two-fold: firstly, they focus on our relationship with God in terms of a loving Father wanting to take care of his children, and secondly on our willingness to accept the role that he may have for us in the outworking of those prayers.

Having met with God through adoration, confession and thanksgiving, we arrive at this place of resubmission. Seeking to put God first and wanting to serve him will guide our petitions towards a balance of self and others. With this new perspective we can understand our own needs better and how to place our requests before God; we have a loving Father who wants us to talk to him about those needs. We can ask God to bless us, heal us, comfort us or guide us; or we can lay more specific problems before him. Here again we can be completely honest, without fear or shame; honest about our thoughts, feelings, desires and hopes.

'Do not be anxious about anything, but
in everything, by prayer and petition,
with thanksgiving, present your requests
to God.'

Philippians 4:6 NIV

Important though our own needs are to God, it is healthy to balance such prayers with intercessions based on world needs. Intercessory supplication can be challenging; it requires us to open ourselves to his will. We must be prepared to be not simply the petitioner, but the vessel for God's answer. In other words, we need to follow prayer with action and action with prayer.

'Let your minds be remade and your
whole nature thus transformed. Then you
will be able to discern the will of God

and know what is good, acceptable and perfect.'

Romans 12:2 NEB

Finally, remember that whatever we ask, we are assured that God will hear us.

'This is the confidence we have in approaching God: that if we ask anything according to his will, he hears us. And if we know that he hears us – whatever we ask – we know that we have what we asked of him.'

1 John 5:14,15 NIV

Using Acts of Prayer

There are 45 pages for each of the A.C.T.S. sections, offering a choice of a Bible verse, a prayer, a quote from a hymn or song or an individual's personal reflective thoughts. We have carefully selected each quote to help you appreciate the depth and variety of meaning within the themes of Adoration, Confession, Thanksgiving and Supplication. It was a challenge to choose quotes that offered a balanced range within each section. The Adoration quotes open our minds to the broad diversity of God's attributes, helping us to be more aware of his nature and consequently creating a greater sense of awe that will inspire us to adore him. The Confession quotes include practical admissions of guilt, a desire to be honest with God who knows our need for forgiveness, and the offer of that forgiveness through Jesus. Thanksgiving quotes include examples of thankfulness, above all for Jesus' sacrifice on the cross and the new start this offers. There is also a variety of examples to encourage us to be thankful for our many blessings. Finally, Supplication quotes reflect the importance of the need to pray for ourselves, for others and for the world, demonstrating God's desire to listen to our petitions while challenging our willingness to be used by him in the working out of these prayers.

There is enough variety in this book to stimulate and encourage you in your journey of faith and to develop your relationship with God. We have used different Bible versions, some with familiar words and others that are more contemporary, in the hope that you will read them in a new and refreshing way. As you work through the progression of A.C.T.S., take time to consider the selected pieces thoughtfully, using the chosen words as a starting point for your own prayers. Choose a page from each section as a platform for your prayers. You can choose the sections beforehand, for example A6, C22, T13 and S1; or you can combine sections in a more structured way, for example A1, C1, T1 and S1 and work through the book systematically. Or, you could open each section of the book randomly as you work through A.C.T.S. However you choose to use the book, it is inevitable that you will pick a quote more than once; do not be put off by this or be tempted to pass it over. We have been using the book during its development and have found that revisiting a quote within a different selection often prompts different responses, thoughts and consequently prayers. We were convinced of the value of the book in helping us to pray imaginatively yet even so were constantly amazed by the way that the sections always seemed to work together. We hope that you too will enjoy the variety of the book and that it will gently guide you in your spiritual journey, drawing you closer to God.

At a Glance

While writing the book we were interested in knowing more about the people behind the quotes. Knowing something of their personality and history made the quotes more meaningful and at times added impact. Putting a face and a context to the words personalised them; for example, S20 is an extract from the hymn *Take My Life and Let It Be* by Frances Ridley Havergal. Although many people will be familiar with these lyrics, not many will know that this hymn was a response to God expressing her joy and thanks when ten house guests gave their lives to Christ after she had prayed for each one of them.

At the back of the book, under the heading *At a Glance*, is an alphabetically ordered selection of biographical details intended to stimulate your interest in the origin of the quotes. They are only glimpses to whet your appetite and although a small number of sources proved elusive, we have collected information on the majority.

Part Two
PRAYER PAGES

Adoration

A1

And God
saw everything
that he had made,
and, behold,
it was very good.

Genesis 1:31a KJV

A2

We can no more diminish God's glory by refusing to worship him than a lunatic can put out the sun by scribbling the word 'darkness' on the walls of his cell . . .

The Problem of Pain C. S. Lewis

A3

I AM
WHO I AM.

Exodus 3:14 NIV(UK)

A4

'To whom will you compare me?
Who is my equal?'
asks the Holy One.

Isaiah 40:25 NLT

A5

Who is like unto thee,
O Lord among Gods?
Who is like unto thee,
glorious in holiness,
fearful in praises,
doing wonders?

Who is like unto thee?

Who Is Like Unto Thee Judy Horner-Montemayor

A6

You alone are God, you were from of old,
and you will be until eternity,
always, first and last,
now and always for ever and ever.

As for you, you are the same,
and your epoch will not come to an end;
as for you, you are the same,
and your kingdom will not be abolished,
and your power is invincible,
and your strength is untiring,
and your magnificence will not be humbled,
and the splendour of your name
   will not be dispelled,
and the praise of your exalted fame
   will not be diminished,
and your light will not be darkened,
and your decree will not be abrogated.

The pillar of your word will not be overthrown,
and your wisdom will not fall into error,
and your counsel will not be concealed.
You alone are God,
   a righteous God over all creation.

Traditional Jewish Prayer translated Margaret Hayon

A7

Of old you laid the foundation of the earth,
and the heavens are the work of your hands.
They will perish, but you will endure;
yes, they will all grow old like a garment;
like a cloak you will change them,
and they will be changed.

But you are the same,
and your years will have no end.

Psalm 102:25-27 NKJV

A8

A true love of God
must begin with a delight in his holiness.

Jonathan Edwards

A9

Within the veil
I now would come,
into the holy place,
to look upon thy face.

I see such beauty there,
no other can compare;
I worship thee, my Lord,
within the veil.

Within the Veil Ruth Dryden

A10

Clothed with splendour and majesty
you wear light like a robe;
the heavens from your sheltering hand unfold.
Awesome God.

You laid the earth on its foundation.
At the sound of your voice
the mountains and oceans took their places.
Awesome God.

All the earth displays your glory,
all creation calls your name.
All of heaven, standing in awe,
all the nations shout your praise.

Creation's anthem will rise to you.
All the universe is crying out for you
in adoration to the Holy One,
in higher praises to the awesome God.

Clothed with Splendour Andy Bromley and Chris Donohue

A11

Glorious are you, more majestic than the everlasting mountains . . .

. . . You are indeed awesome!

Psalm 76:4,7a NRSV

A12

You are holy, Lord, the only God,
and your deeds are wonderful.
You are strong. You are great.
You are the Most High. You are almighty.
You, Holy Father, are King of heaven and earth.
You are Three and One, Lord God, all good.
You are good, all good, supreme good,
Lord God, living and true.
You are love. You are wisdom.
You are humility. You are endurance.
You are rest. You are peace.
You are joy and gladness.
You are justice and moderation.
You are all our riches, and you suffice for us.
You are beauty. You are gentleness.
You are our protector.
You are our guardian and defender.
You are our courage.
You are our haven and our hope.
You are our faith, our great consolation.
You are our eternal life, great and
  wonderful Lord,
God almighty, merciful Saviour.

St Francis of Assisi

A13

And on it stood all the people who had
been victorious over the beast and his statue
and the number representing his name.
They were all holding harps that God had
given them. And they were singing the song
of Moses, the servant of God, and the song
of the Lamb:
'Great and marvellous are your works,
O Lord God, the almighty.
Just and true are your ways, O King of
the nations.
Who will not fear you, Lord, and glorify
your name?
For you alone are holy.
All nations will come and worship before you,
for your righteous deeds have been revealed.'

Revelation 15:2b-4 NLT

A14

Praising God is one of the highest and
purest acts of religion.

In prayer we act like human beings,
in praise we act like angels.

Thomas John Watson

A15

Praise be to you, O Lord,
God of our Father Israel,
from everlasting to everlasting.
Yours, O Lord, is the greatness and
  the power
  and the glory and the majesty
  and the splendour,
for everything in heaven and earth is yours.
Yours, O Lord, is the kingdom.

You are exalted as head over all.

1 Chronicles 29:10, 11 NIV(UK)

A16

For the love of God is broader than the
measure of our mind;
and the heart of the Eternal is most
wonderfully kind.

There's a Wideness in God's Mercy Frederick W. Faber

A17

Powerful, so powerful,
your glory fills the skies,
your mighty works displayed for all to see.
The beauty of your majesty awakes my
heart to sing
how marvellous, how wonderful you are.

You opened my eyes to your wonders anew,
you captured my heart with this love,
because nothing on earth is as beautiful
as you.

Beautiful One Tim Hughes

A18

How rich and deep are the wisdom and
 the knowledge of God!
We cannot reach to the root of his decisions
 or his ways.
Who has ever known the mind of the Lord?
Who has ever been his advisor?
Who has given anything to him,
so that his presents came only as a
 debt returned?
Everything there is comes from him
and is caused by him and exists for him.

To him be glory for ever! Amen.

Romans 11:33-36 NJB

A19

O worship the Lord
in the beauty of holiness,
bow down before him,
his glory proclaim;
with gold of obedience
and incense of lowliness,
kneel and adore him,
the Lord is his name.

O Worship the Lord J. S. B. Monsell

A20

Can you understand the mysteries
  surrounding God all-powerful?
They are higher than the heavens
  and deeper than the grave.

So what can you do when you know so little
and these mysteries outreach the earth and
  the ocean?

Job 11:7-9 CEV

A21

I will praise you, O Lord, among the nations;
I will sing of you among the peoples.
For great is your love, higher than the heavens,
your faithfulness reaches to the skies.
Be exalted, O God, above the heavens,
and let your glory be over all the earth.

Psalm 108:3-5 NIV(UK)

A22

When I go aside in order to pray, I find my heart unwilling to approach God; and when I tarry in prayer my heart is unwilling to abide in him.
Therefore I am compelled first to pray to God to move my heart into himself, and when I am in him, I pray that my heart remain in him.

John Bunyan

A23

Ascribe greatness to our God, the Rock,
his work is perfect
and all his ways are just.

A God of faithfulness
and without injustice,
good and upright is he.

Ascribe Greatness
Mary Kirkbride-Barthow and Mary Lou King

A24

Who would not revere you,
King of nations?
Yes, this is your due.
Since, of all the wise among the nations,
and in all their kingdoms,
there is not a single one like you.

Jeremiah 10:7 NJB

A25

Your unfailing love, O Lord, is as vast as
the heavens;
your faithfulness reaches beyond the clouds.

Your righteousness is like the mighty
mountains,
your justice like the ocean depths.

Psalm 36:5,6 NLT

A26

I want deliberately to encourage this mighty longing after God. The lack of it has brought us to our present low estate. The stiff and wooden quality about our religious lives is a result of our lack of holy desire . . .

. . . He waits to be wanted. Too bad that with many of us he waits so long, so very long, in vain.

The Pursuit of God A. W. Tozer

A27

Holy, holy, holy
is the Lord God, the Almighty;
he was, he is and he is to come.

Revelation 4:8b JB

A28

My God, how wonderful you are,
your majesty how bright!
How beautiful your mercy-seat,
in depths of burning light!

How wonderful, how beautiful,
your loving face must be,
your endless wisdom, boundless power
and awesome purity!

My God, How Wonderful You Are Frederick W. Faber

A29

Blessed are you, Lord our God,
king of the universe!
Your word brings on the dusk at evening,
your wisdom creates both night and day.
You determine the cycles of time,
arrange the succession of seasons,
and establish the stars in their heavenly courses.
Lord of the starry hosts is your name.
Living and eternal God,
rule over us always.
Blessed be the Lord,
whose word makes evening fall.
Amen.

Jewish Evening Prayer

A30

I am dwelling on the mountain,
where the golden sunlight gleams
o'er a land whose wondrous beauty,
far exceeds my fondest dreams;
where the air is pure, ethereal,
laden with the breath of flow'rs,
they are blooming by the fountain,
'neath the amaranthine bow'rs.

Anon.

A31

He alone stretches out the heavens
and treads on the waves of the sea.

He is the Maker of the Bear and Orion,
the Pleiades and the constellations of
the south.

He performs wonders that cannot be
fathomed,
miracles that cannot be counted.

Job 9:8-10 NIV(UK)

A32

We declare your majesty,
we proclaim that your name is exalted;
for you reign magnificently, rule victoriously,
and your power is shown
throughout the earth.

And we exclaim our God is mighty,
lift up your name, for you are holy.

Sing it again, all honour and glory,
in adoration we bow before your throne.

We Declare Your Majesty Malcolm du Plessis

A33

Lord God, so many words are used to
describe you,
in an attempt to sum up just who and
what you are.
We speak of your power, might and majesty
to express your greatness.
We label you eternal, everlasting, infinite,
to convey your timelessness.
We speak of your justice, righteousness and
holiness to encapsulate your otherness.
We call you Creator, Father, Redeemer
to articulate your goodness.
Yet, all these words fall short, pointing to
part but not all of the truth.
I praise you, though, that there is one word
that says it all – that little word 'love'.
Overworked, misapplied, misunderstood
it may be, but it is your whole nature,
your whole purpose and your whole being.

A34

Almighty God,
whose glory the heavens are telling,
the earth thy power,
the sea thy might,
and whose greatness all feeling and
  thinking creatures everywhere proclaim:
to thee belongeth glory, honour,
might and magnificence,
now and for ever,
unto the ages of ages.

After St James

A35

O Lord, our Lord,
how majestic is your name
in all the earth!
You have set your glory
above the heavens.

Psalm 8:1 NIV(UK)

A36

Our Lord, you are King!
Majesty and power are your royal robes.
You put the world in place,
and it will never be moved.
You have always ruled,
and you are eternal.
The ocean is roaring, Lord!
The sea is pounding hard.
Its mighty waves are majestic,
but you are more majestic,
and you rule over all.
Your decisions are firm,
and your temple will always be beautiful
 and holy.

Psalm 93 CEV

A37

Truth and righteousness enthrone him,
just and equal are his ways;
more than happy, those who own him,
more than joy, their song of praise!
Sun and shield and great reward:

Who is like him?

Praise the Lord!

Timeless Love! We Sing the Story Timothy Dudley-Smith

A38

He has made everything beautiful
in its time.
He has put thoughts of the forever in
our mind,
yet we cannot understand the work
God has done from the beginning
to the end.

Ecclesiastes 3:11 NLV

A39

Blessed are you, Adonai our God,
ruler of the universe,
who forms light and creates darkness,
makes peace and creates all . . .
. . . How great are your works, Adonai.
You make them all with wisdom,
the world is full of your possessions.
May you be blessed, Adonai our God,
beyond the praises of your handiwork
and beyond the brilliant lights that you made.
May they themselves glorify you.
Blessed are you, Adonai,
creator of the lights.

Adapted from a Jewish Morning Prayer

A40

The steadfast love of the Lord never ceases;
his mercies never come to an end;
they are new every morning:

Great is your faithfulness.

Lamentations 3:22, 23 ESV

A41

The warmth of the sun's embrace,
the gentle breeze swept in by incoming tide,
the rhythm of seasons of new birth,
death and recreation.
All these speak so clearly of your love,
your power and your beauty.
All are expressions of your creativity and
  more importantly of yourself.
As an artist might share his personality
  within each brushstroke,
so within the myriad colours of a butterfly's
  wing you share the exuberance of your love.

John Birch

A42

O Lord, you are my God;
I will exalt you and praise your name,
for in perfect faithfulness you have done
  marvellous things,
things planned long ago.

Isaiah 25:1 NIV(UK)

A43

'Am I only a God nearby,' declares the Lord, 'and not a God far away?

Can anyone hide in secret places so that I cannot see him?' declares the Lord.

'Do not I fill heaven and earth?' declares the Lord.

Jeremiah 23:23, 24 NIV(UK)

A44

Loving God means rejoicing in God,
being eager to think of and pray to God.
It means being glad to be in God's
presence and to be with God alone.

It means not grieving God,
but rejoicing in God simply because it is
God who is involved,
and because we are permitted to know
and have God,
and to speak with and live with God.

Dietrich Bonhoeffer

A45

This is the place where dreams are found,
where vision comes, called holy ground.
Your fire burns but never dies;
I realise this is holy ground.

The Great I Am, revealed to us;
take off your shoes, this is holy ground.

This Is the Place Dave Bilbrough

Confession

C1

You yourselves are a case study of
what he does.
At one time you all had your backs turned
to God, thinking rebellious thoughts of him,
giving him trouble every chance you got.
But now, by giving himself completely
at the cross, actually dying for you,
Christ brought you over to God's side and
put your lives together, whole and holy
in his presence.
You don't walk away from a gift like that!
You stay grounded and steady in that
bond of trust,
constantly tuned in to the message,
careful not to be distracted or diverted.
There is no other message – just this one.
Every creature under heaven gets this
same message.
I, Paul, am a messenger of this message.

Colossians 1:21-23 TM

C2

If we do things to please
  our sinful old self,
our soul will be lost.

If we do things to please
  the Holy Spirit,
we will have life that lasts forever.

Galatians 6:8 NLV

C3

Dear Lord and Father of mankind,
forgive our foolish ways;
reclothe us in our rightful mind;
in purer lives thy service find,
in deeper reverence, praise,
in deeper reverence, praise.

Dear Lord and Father of Mankind John G. Whittier

C4

Merciful God,
I come to you today with a humble heart.
I am in need.
I am in need of your understanding and forgiveness.
I am in need of your mercy and grace.
And I am in need of your compassion and love.
I know I don't really deserve any of these things.
In so many ways, I fall far short every day.
I'm not always understanding with those around me,
and I don't always forgive others the way I should.
But I also realise that your understanding and forgiveness are not reserved solely for those who 'deserve' them.
They are always free for the asking.
You offer compassion and love to anyone who comes to you with an open heart.
Please know that my heart is open wide today.

Prayers from the Heart
Used with permission.

C5

You must give your whole heart to him
and hold out your hands to him for help.

Put away the sin that is in your hand;
let no evil remain in your tent.

Then you can lift up your face
    without shame,
and you can stand strong without fear.

Job 11:13-15 TYB

C6

The bridge of grace will bear your weight,
brother.
Thousands of big sinners have gone across
that bridge,
yea, tens of thousands have gone over it.
I can hear their trampings now
as they traverse the great arches of the
bridge of salvation.
They come by the thousands,
by their myriads,
ere since that day when Christ first entered
his glory.
They come and yet never a stone has
sprung in that mighty bridge.
Some have been the chief of sinners
and some have come at the very last of
their days,
but the arch has never yielded beneath
their weight.
I will go with them, trusting to the
same support.
It will bear me over as it has for them.

Charles H. Spurgeon

C7

At the foot of the cross
I found Jesus.
At the foot of the cross
I found healing.
At the foot of the cross
I found peace and joy within.

Broke the bonds of binding sin,
saw God's plan for fallen ones.
Now I live for him alone,
for my sins he did atone
when I knelt at the foot of the cross.

At the Foot of the Cross Freda Lindsay

C8

We worship at your feet,
where wrath and mercy meet,
and a guilty world is washed by
  love's pure stream.
For us he was made sin –
oh help me take it in.
Deep wounds of love cry out
'Father, forgive'.
I worship, I worship,
the Lamb who was slain.

We Worship at Your Feet Graham Kendrick

C9

I have come to call not the righteous
but sinners to repentance.

Luke 5:32 NRSV

C10

Dear Heavenly Father,

There's nothing else to say but 'I'm sorry'.
I know we've been down this road before.
My heart wants to promise perfection.
I want to believe that this is the last time
I'll ever blow it.
But, that isn't the reality of my life.
Every day is a battle.
I struggle between following you and
choosing what feels right at the moment.
I need your wisdom and power to persevere
towards a true change of heart and action.
But, most of all, I need your forgiveness.

Thank you for asking Jesus to pay the
high price for what I've done.
The thought of his sacrifice
and your unending grace
humbles me beyond words.
'Thank you' will never be enough.

Life's Daily Prayer Book for Women
Used by permission of Thomas Nelson Gift Books

C11

I have swept away your sins
  like the morning mists.
I have scattered your offences
  like the clouds.
Oh return to me,
for I have paid the price to set you free.
Sing, O heavens, for the Lord
  has done this wondrous thing.
Shout, O earth!
Break forth into song,
O mountains and forests and every tree!
For the Lord has redeemed Jacob
and is glorified in Israel.

Isaiah 44:22, 23 NLT

C12

Confess yourself to heaven,
repent what's past,
avoid what is to come,
and do not spread the compost on
the weeds to make them ranker.

Hamlet William Shakespeare

C13

Say a quiet 'yes' to God
and he'll be there in no time.

Quit dabbling in sin.
Purify your inner life.
Quit playing the field.

James 4:8 TM

C14

Rock of ages, cleft for me,
let me hide myself in thee;
let the water and the blood,
from thy riven side which flowed,
be of sin the double cure,
cleanse me from its guilt and power.

Nothing in my hands I bring,
simply to thy cross I cling;
naked, come to thee for dress;
helpless, look to thee for grace;
foul, I to the fountain fly:
wash me, Saviour, or I die.

Rock of Ages Augustus Montague Toplady

C15

I heard that you were here,
sweet hope to the ear of the ones
  heavy-laden with their sin.
I heard that you have time for the lame
  and the blind,
for those who need a Saviour as much as me.

And so I have come, I have come to the One
with the power to condemn or forgive.
And so I have come, I have come to the One
who restores a life again to be relived.

With a broken heart I kneel,
with a broken heart I kneel,
I'll wash your feet with my tears,
for the sins of the years,
yet tears in need of washing by you.
I'll break the alabaster vial
bought with blackness and vile
and lavish bittersweet perfume on you.

With a broken heart I kneel,
with a broken heart I kneel,
and everyone will know,
through nothing of my own
by your goodness alone,
you love me where I kneel.

I Kneel Paul Landers

C16

So get rid of every kind of evil.
Stop telling lies.
Don't pretend to be something you are not.
Stop wanting what others have.
Don't speak against each other.
Like babies that were just born,
you should long for the pure milk
  of God's word.
It will help you grow up as believers.
You can do it now that you have tasted
  how good the Lord is.

1 Peter 2:1-3 NIRV

C17

God is sheer mercy and grace;
not easily angered, he's rich in love.

He doesn't endlessly nag and scold,
nor hold grudges forever.
He doesn't treat us as our sins deserve,
nor pay us back in full for our wrongs.

As high as heaven is over the earth,
so strong is his love to those who fear him.
And as far as sunrise is from sunset,
he has separated us from our sins.

Psalm 103:8-12 TM

C18

If I have wounded any soul today,
if I have caused one foot to go astray,
if I have walked in my own willful way,
Good Lord, forgive!

If I have uttered idle words or vain,
if I have turned aside from want or pain,
lest I myself should suffer through the strain,
Good Lord, forgive!

If I have craved for joys that are not mine,
if I have let my wayward heart repine,
dwelling on things of earth, not things divine,
Good Lord, forgive!

If I have been perverse, or hard, or cold,
if I have longed for shelter in thy fold,
when thou has given me some part to hold,
Good Lord, forgive!

Forgive the sins I have confessed to thee,
forgive the secret sins I do not see,
that which I know not, Father, teach thou me.
Help me to live.

An Evening Prayer Maud Battersby

C19

. . . God's not interested in operating a brownie-point system – he's only interested in loving and forgiving those who are brave enough not to deny what they've done, no matter how terrible, brave enough to be truly sorry, brave enough to resolve to make a fresh start in serving him as well as they possibly can.

A Question of Integrity Susan Howatch

C20

Either sin is with you, lying on your
 shoulders,
or it is lying on Christ, the Lamb of God.

Now if it is lying on your back,
 you are lost;

but if it is resting on Christ, you are free,
 and you will be saved.

Now choose what you want.

Martin Luther

C21

God of grace,

I turn my face to you, I cannot hide.
My nakedness, my shame, my guilt are all
before your eyes.
Strivings and all anguished dreams in rags
lie at my feet,
and only grace provides the way
for me to stand complete.

And your grace clothes me in
righteousness,
and your mercy covers me in love.
Your life adorns and beautifies.
I stand complete in you.

God of Grace Chris Bowater

C22

Who can say, 'I have made my heart clean;
I am pure from my sin?'

Proverbs 20:9 RSV

C23

I'm on my knees at the cross,
where your blood was sacrificed,
so amazed, that there is grace enough for me.
I don't deserve the love you bring,
but I'm in that place again
where I need you to forgive my foolish heart.
Oh what mercy, oh what mercy,
oh what mercy is mine to receive.

I'm On My Knees Dave Bilbrough

C24

Almighty and most merciful Father,

we have wandered and strayed from your
ways like lost sheep.
We have followed too much the devices
and desires of our own hearts.
We have offended against your holy laws.
We have left undone those things that we
ought to have done;
and we have done those things that we
ought not to have done;
and there is no health in us.

But you, O Lord, have mercy upon us sinners.
Spare those who confess their faults.
Restore those who are penitent,
according to your promises declared to
humankind in Christ Jesus our Lord.

And grant, O most merciful Father,
for his sake,
that we may live a disciplined,
righteous, and godly life,
to the glory of your holy name.
Amen.

A General Confession, Book of Common Prayer

C25

People who cover over their sins
   will not prosper.
But if they confess and forsake them,
they will receive mercy.

Proverbs 28:13 NLT

C26

No more hiding in the shadows ashamed
  to show my face,
unwilling to accept the blame of my disgrace.
My stinging tongue, my stubborn mind,
my guilty hands and leaden feet,
are laid before my God in sorrow
  when we meet.
But I know that God forgives me for those
  things I've said and done.
I'm sure that he forgives me,
that's why he sent his Son;
Christ's blood revives my wizened heart,
firm promise of a fresh new start
  when I say 'Sorry, Lord.
This time it's true; I'm turning back to you.'

Anon.

C27

I thank him who has given me strength,
Christ Jesus our Lord,
because he judged me faithful,
appointing me to his service,
though formerly I was a blasphemer,
persecutor, and insolent opponent.
But I received mercy because I had acted
  ignorantly in unbelief,
and the grace of our Lord overflowed for me
with the faith and love that are in
Christ Jesus.
The saying is trustworthy
and deserving of full acceptance,
that Christ Jesus came into the world to
  save sinners,
of whom I am the foremost.
But I received mercy for this reason,
that in me, as the foremost,
Jesus Christ might display his perfect patience
as an example to those who were to believe
  in him for eternal life.

1 Timothy 1:12-16 ESV

C28

When Satan tempts me to despair
and tells me of the guilt within,
upward I look and see him there,
who made an end to all my sin.
Because the sinless Saviour died,
my sinful soul is counted free;
for God the just is satisfied
to look on him and pardon me.

Before the Throne of God Above Charitie L. Bancroft

C29

. . . everything – and I do mean everything –
connected with that old way of life has to go.
It's rotten through and through.
Get rid of it! And then take on an entirely
new way of life – a God-fashioned life,
life renewed from the inside
and working itself into your conduct
as God accurately reproduces his character
in you.
What this adds up to, then, is this:
no more lies, no more pretence.
Tell your neighbour the truth.
In Christ's body we're all connected to each
other, after all.
When you lie to others, you end up lying
to yourself.
Go ahead and be angry.
You do well to be angry –
but don't use your anger as fuel for revenge.
And don't stay angry.
Don't go to bed angry.
Don't give the devil that kind of foothold
in your life.

Don't grieve God.
Don't break his heart.
His Holy Spirit,
moving and breathing in you,
is the most intimate part of your life,
making you fit for himself.
Don't take such a gift for granted.
Make a clean break with all cutting,
  backbiting, profane talk.
Be gentle with one another, sensitive.
Forgive one another as quickly and
  thoroughly as God in Christ forgave you.

Ephesians 4:20-32 TM

C30

There is not a righteous person on earth
who does what is right and never sins.

Ecclesiastes 7:20 NIV(UK)

C31

Forgive me my sins, O Lord:
the sins of my present
  and the sins of my past,
the sins of my soul
  and the sins of my body.

Forgive my casual sins
  and my deliberate sins,
and those which I have
  laboured so long to hide
that I have hidden them,
  even from myself.

Forgive me them, O Lord,
forgive them all,
for the sake of Jesus Christ my Saviour.

Bishop Thomas Wilson

C32

At last I admitted to you I had sinned;
no longer concealing my guilt, I said,

'I will go to Yahweh and confess my fault.'

And you,
you have forgiven the wrong I did,
have pardoned my sin.

Psalm 32:5 JB

C33

River, wash over me,

cleanse me and make me new.
Bathe me, refresh me and fill me anew,

river, wash over me.

River Wash Over Me Dougie Brown

C34

Turn away from your sins!
Turn away from all of the evil things
  you have done.
Then sin will not bring you down.
Get rid of all of the evil things
  you have done.

Let me give you a new heart
  and a new spirit.
Then you will be faithful to me.

Ezekiel 18:30b, 31 NIRV

C35

A person's very highest moment is,
I have no doubt at all,
when they kneel in the dust,
and beat their breast,
and tell all the sins of their life.

De Profundis Oscar Wilde

C36

I am trusting thee, Lord Jesus,
trusting only thee!
Trusting thee for full salvation,
great and free.

I am trusting thee for pardon,
at thy feet I bow;
for thy grace and tender mercy,
trusting now.

I am trusting thee for cleansing
in the crimson flood;
trusting thee to make me holy,
by thy blood.

I Am Trusting Thee, Lord Jesus Frederick W. Faber

C37

Change your hearts and lives because
the kingdom of heaven is near.

Matthew 3:2 TYB

C38

Breathe on me, Breath of God,
until my heart is pure;
until my will is one with thine
to do and to endure.

Breathe on me, Breath of God,
till I am wholly thine;
until this earthly part of me
glows with thy fire divine.

Breathe on Me, Breath of God Edwin Hatch

C39

But God had so much loving-kindness.
He loved us with such a great love.
Even when we were dead
because of our sins,
he made us alive
by what Christ did for us.
You have been saved from the punishment
of sin by his loving-favour.
God raised us up from death
when he raised up Christ Jesus.
He has given us a place
with Christ in the heavens.
He did this to show us
through all the time to come
the great riches of his loving-favour.
He has shown us his kindness
through Christ Jesus.

For by his loving-favour you have been
saved from the punishment of sin
through faith.
It is not by anything you have done.
It is a gift of God.
It is not given to you
because you worked for it.
If you could work for it,
you would be proud.
We are his work.
He has made us to belong to Christ Jesus
so we can work for him.
He planned that we should do this.

Ephesians 2:4-10 NLV

C40

The grace of God means something like:

Here is your life.
You might never have been, but you are
  because the party wouldn't have been
  complete without you.
Here is the world.
Beautiful and terrible things will happen.
Don't be afraid. I am with you.
Nothing can ever separate us.
It's for you I created the universe.
I love you.
There's only one catch.
Like any other gift, the gift of grace can be
  yours only if you'll reach out and take it.
Maybe being able to reach out and take it
  is a gift too.

Carl Frederick Buechner

C41

Come now, and let us reason together,
saith the Lord: though your sins be as
scarlet, they shall be as white as snow;
though they be red like crimson,
they shall be as wool.

Isaiah 1:18 KJV

C42

Forgive us, God,
for what we did in carelessness and haste;
we never did intend to cause such damage
and such waste.

So, as in sorrow we repent,
we ask on bended knee to give us, God,
the strength now to restore the earth for thee.

Revd Bill McGinnis

C43

Just as I am, without one plea,
but that thy blood was shed for me,
and that thou bid'st me come to thee,
O Lamb of God, I come.

Just as I am, and waiting not
to rid my soul of one dark blot,
to thee, whose blood can cleanse each spot,
O Lamb of God, I come.

Just as I am, thou wilt receive,
wilt welcome, pardon, cleanse, relieve,
because thy promise I believe,
O Lamb of God, I come.

Just as I Am Charlotte Elliot

C44

Who is a God like you, who pardons sin
and forgives the transgression of the
  remnant of his inheritance?
You do not stay angry for ever
  but delight to show mercy.
You will again have compassion on us;
you will tread our sins underfoot
and hurl all our iniquities into the depths
  of the sea.

Micah 7:18, 19 NIV(UK)

C45

If we say we have no sin in us,
we are deceiving ourselves and refusing
to admit the truth;
but if we acknowledge our sins,
then God, who is faithful and just,
will forgive our sins and purify us from
everything that is wrong.

1 John 1:8, 9 JB

Thanksgiving

T1

You did not wait for me to draw near to you,
but you clothed yourself with frail humanity.

You did not wait for me to cry out to you,
but you let me hear your voice calling me.

And I'm forever grateful to you,
I'm forever grateful for the cross.
I'm forever grateful to you,
that you came to seek and save the lost.

I'm Forever Grateful Mark Altrogge

T2

All the angels were standing
around the throne
and around the leaders and the four
living beings.
They bowed down their faces in front
of the throne and worshipped God.
They said, 'May it be so!
Blessing, praise, glory and wisdom,
thanks, honour, power, and strength
belong to our God for ever and ever!
Amen!'

Revelation 7:11, 12 WWE(NT)

T3

We praise you for the wider church
of which we are a part,
for Christians of different countries
and cultures,
each working out their faith in a multitude
of places and situations.
We thank you for all that we can learn
from them,
for the examples they give of courage and
perseverance,
vision and commitment, mission
and service,
fellowship and worship.

T4

I am a new creation,
no more in condemnation,
here in the grace of God I stand.
My heart is overflowing,
my love just keeps on growing,
here in the grace of God I stand.
And I will praise you, Lord,
yes I will praise you, Lord,
and I will sing of all that you have done.
A joy that knows no limit,
a lightness in my spirit –
here in the grace of God I stand.

I Am a New Creation Dave Bilbrough

T5

Son of God, you reign in heaven's glory,
yet you chose to come to earth and save me.
Humbled yourself to die the cruellest death.
No other act of love compares to this.

The greatest gift I've ever received is
  the cross, the cross.
For there you gave yourself up for me,
  on the cross, the cross,
and with the blood you poured out for me
  you have saved my soul.
You have given me the greatest gift of all.

Your heart aches for all the lost and hurting,
at the cross you wait to take our burdens,
longing to heal our wounds
  and make us whole,
longing to hear us sing with thankful souls.

The Greatest Gift Vicky Beeching

T6

Be joyful always; pray continually;
give thanks in all circumstances,
for this is God's will for you
in Christ Jesus.

1 Thessalonians 5:16-18 NIV(UK)

T7

Far away in the depths of my spirit tonight
rolls a melody sweeter than psalm;
in celestial-like strains it unceasingly falls
o'er my soul like an infinite calm.

What a treasure I have in the wonderful peace,
buried deep in the heart of my soul,
so secure that no power can mine it away
while the years of eternity roll.

Wonderful Peace Warren D. Cornell

T8

At times our own light goes out and is rekindled by a spark from another person. Each of us has cause to think with deep gratitude of those who have lighted the flame within us.

Albert Schweitzer

T9

Let never day nor night unhallowed pass
but still remember what the Lord hath done.

King Henry VI William Shakespeare

T10

Dear brothers and sisters,
we can't help but thank God for you,
because your faith is flourishing
and your love for one another is growing.

2 Thessalonians 1:3 NLT

T11

You laid aside your majesty,
gave up everything for me,
suffered at the hands of those
  you had created.
You took all my guilt and shame,
when you died and rose again,
now today you reign,
in heaven and earth exalted.

I really want to worship you, my Lord,
you have won my heart and I am yours
for ever and ever; I will love you.
You are the only one who died for me,
gave your life to set me free,
so I lift my voice to you in adoration.

You Laid Aside Your Majesty Noel Richards

T12

As Jesus took the five loaves of bread and two fish, he looked up to heaven and gave thanks. He broke them in pieces and gave them to his followers to give to the people.

Luke 9:16 NLV

T13

O Lord, my God!

When I in awesome wonder
consider all the works thy hand hath made,
I see the stars, I hear the mighty thunder,
thy power throughout the universe
displayed.

And when I think that God, his Son not
sparing,
sent him to die – I scarce can take it in,
that on the cross my burden gladly bearing,
he bled and died to take away my sin:

Then sings my soul,
my Saviour God, to thee,
how great thou art, how great thou art!

O Lord, My God! Stuart K. Hine

T14

When the builders had finished laying the
   foundation of the temple,
the priests put on their robes and blew
   trumpets in honour of the Lord,
while the Levites from the family of Asaph
   praised God with cymbals.
All of them followed the instructions given
   years before by King David.
They praised the Lord and gave thanks as
   they took turns singing:
'The Lord is good!
His faithful love for Israel will last forever.'
Everyone started shouting and praising
   the Lord because work on the
   foundation of the temple had begun.
Many of the older priests and Levites and
   the heads of families cried aloud
   because they remembered seeing the
   first temple years before.
But others were so happy that they
   celebrated with joyful shouts.

Ezra 3:10-12 CEV

T15

The God of the universe sees me!
Lord, I'm absolutely in awe that you not only see the outside of me, but you also see the inside.
You know my innermost thoughts and feelings, you know when I'm hurting, you know when I'm happy, you know when I need the touch of your gentle hand the most.
Lord, thank you for caring about me so intimately.

Joni Eareckson Tada

T16

Those who bring thanksgiving
as their sacrifice honour me.

Psalm 50:14 NRSV

T17

For the rest of my life I'm going to trust that God is always at work in all things, and give him thanks long before my simplest prayers are answered.

Nancy Parker Brummett

T18

For each new morning with its light,
for rest and shelter of the night,
for health and food,
for love and friends,
for everything thy goodness sends.

Ralph Waldo Emerson

T19

In that day you will say:
'Give thanks to the Lord, call on his name;
make known among the nations
  what he has done,
and proclaim that his name is exalted.
Sing to the Lord, for he has done glorious
  things;
let this be known to all the world.
Shout aloud and sing for joy,
  people of Zion,
for great is the Holy One of Israel
  among you.'

Isaiah 12:4-6 NIV(UK)

T20

We could watch you from afar,
and forever be amazed at how glorious
you are.
Yet you've drawn us close to you,
where the wonder's greater still,
and you overwhelm us, God.

And we rejoice with trembling in our hearts,
bring you a song of reverence and love.
Jesus, how good, how great you are
and we rejoice with trembling before
your throne.

Rejoice With Trembling Matt Redman

T21

Almighty God, Creator and Redeemer,
we praise you for your work of creation;
for the beauty of the world around us
and for every gift we enjoy.
We bless you for creating us to know you,
love you and obey you.

Amen.

T22

What a God we have!

And how fortunate we are to have him,
this Father of our master Jesus!
Because Jesus was raised from the dead,
we've been given a brand-new life
and have everything to live for,
including a future in heaven –
and the future starts now!
God is keeping careful watch over us
  and the future.
The day is coming when you'll have it all –
life healed and whole.
I know how great this makes you feel,
even though you have to put up with every
  kind of aggravation in the meantime.
Pure gold put in the fire comes out of it
  proved pure;
genuine faith put through this suffering
  comes out proved genuine.
When Jesus wraps this all up, it's your faith,
  not your gold that God will have on
  display as evidence of his victory.

1 Peter 1:3-7 TM

T23

Then Mary said, 'My heart sings with thanks for my Lord. And my spirit is happy in God, the one who saves from the punishment of sin. The Lord has looked on me, his servant-girl and one who is not important. But from now on all people will honour me. He who is powerful has done great things for me. His name is holy. The loving-kindness of the Lord is given to the people of all times who honour him. He has done powerful works with his arm. He has divided from each other those who have pride in their hearts. He has taken rulers down from their thrones. He has put those who are in a place that is not important to a place that is important. He has filled those who are hungry with good things. He has sent the rich people away with nothing. He has helped Israel his servant. This was done to remember his loving-kindness. He promised he would do this to our early fathers and to Abraham and to his family forever.'

Luke 1:46-55 NLV

T24

I may not be where I want to be,
but thank God
I'm not where I used to be.

T25

Jesus was going on the road to Jerusalem. He went between the countries of Samaria and Galilee. When he was going into a village, ten men who had leprosy came to him. They stood far away. And they called out, 'Jesus, master, help us!' When Jesus saw them, he said to them, 'Go and let the priests look at you.' While they were going, they were healed of the leprosy. One of them, when he saw that he was healed, turned back. He praised God with a loud voice. He bowed down in front of Jesus and thanked him. He was a man from the country of Samaria. Then Jesus asked, 'Were not ten people healed? Where are the other nine? Is this stranger the only one who has come back to praise God?' Then he said to the man, 'Get up and go on your way. You were healed because you believed.'

Luke 17:11-19 WWE(NT)

T26

Amazing grace!
How sweet the sound
that saved a wretch like me;
I once was lost, but now am found,
was blind but now I see.

Amazing Grace John Newton

T27

Jesus Christ,

I think upon your sacrifice,
you became nothing, poured out to death.
Many times I've wondered at
  your gift of life,
and I'm in that place once again.

And once again I look upon the cross
  where you died,
I'm humbled by your mercy and I'm
  broken inside.

Once again I thank you,
once again I pour out my life.

Once Again Matt Redman

T28

I know how to live when I am poor,
and I know how to live when I have plenty.
I have learned the secret of being happy
  at any time in everything that happens,
when I have enough to eat and
  when I go hungry,
when I have more than I need and
  when I do not have enough.
I can do all things through Christ,
because he gives me strength.
But it was good that you helped me
  when I needed it.

Philippians 4:12-14 TYB

T29

The fig trees might not bud.
The vines might not produce any grapes.
The olive crop might fail.
The fields might not produce any food.
There might not be any sheep in the pens.
There might not be any cattle in the barns.
But
I will still be glad because of what the Lord
has done.
God my Saviour fills me with joy.
The Lord and King gives me strength.
He makes my feet like the feet of a deer.
He helps me walk on the highest places.

Habakkuk 3:17-19 NIRV

T30

For food that stays our hunger,
for rest that brings us ease,
for homes where memories linger,
we give our thanks for these.

Traditional Mealtime Blessing

T31

O God, we thank thee for this universe,
  our great home;
for its vastness and its riches,
and for the manifoldness of the life which
  teems upon it
and of which we are part.

We praise thee for the arching sky and the
  blessed winds,
for the driving clouds and the constellations
  on high.

We praise thee for the salt sea and the
  running water,
for the everlasting hills, for the trees,
and for the grass under our feet.

We thank thee for our senses by which we
  can see the splendour of the morning,
and hear the jubilant songs of love,
and smell the breath of the springtime.

Walter Rauschenbusch

T32

I awoke this morning with devout
thanksgiving for my friends,
the old and new.

Ralph Waldo Emerson

T33

Now thanks be to God who always leads us in triumph in Christ, and through us diffuses the fragrance of his knowledge in every place.

2 Corinthians 2:14 NKJV

T34

I thank you, Lord,
for hearing all my prayers,
for taking time to listen to my pleas,
for taking action, when you thought it best,
and for withholding, when the time was wrong.
As shepherd to his sheep you are to me,
and I am happy being in your fold.
In Jesus' holy name I pray.
Amen.

Revd Bill McGinnis

T35

Here is love vast as the ocean,
loving kindness as the flood,
when the Prince of Life, our ransom,
shed for us his precious blood.

Who his love will not remember?
Who can cease to sing his praise?
He can never be forgotten
throughout heaven's eternal days.

On the mount of crucifixion
fountains opened deep and wide;
through the floodgates of God's mercy
flowed a vast and gracious tide.

Grace and love, like mighty rivers,
poured incessant from above,
and heaven's peace and perfect justice
kissed a guilty world in love.

Here is Love, Vast as the Ocean William Rees
(trans. William Edwards, 1900)

T36

Tell out, my soul, the greatness of the Lord;
unnumbered blessings give my spirit voice;
tender to me the promise of his word;
in God my Saviour shall my heart rejoice.

Tell out, my soul, the greatness of his name!

Tell out, my soul, the greatness of his might!

Tell out, my soul, the glories of his word!
Firm is his promise, and his mercy sure;
tell out, my soul, the greatness of the Lord
to children's children and for evermore!

Tell Out My Soul Timothy Dudley-Smith

T37

And let the peace of Christ rule in your hearts, to which indeed you were called in one body. And be thankful. Let the word of Christ dwell in you richly, teaching and admonishing one another in all wisdom, singing psalms and hymns and spiritual songs, with thankfulness in your hearts to God. And whatever you do, in word or deed, do everything in the name of the Lord Jesus, giving thanks to God the Father through him.

Colossians 3:15-17 ESV

T38

Even though I clutch my blanket and
growl when the alarm rings each morning,
thank you, Lord, that I can hear.
There are many who are deaf.

Even though I keep my eyes tightly closed
against the morning light as long as possible,
thank you, Lord, that I can see.
There are many who are blind.

Even though I huddle in my bed and put
off the effort of rising,
thank you, Lord, that I have the strength
to rise.
There are many who are bedridden.

Even though the first hour of my day is
hectic, when socks are lost, toast is burned,
and tempers are short,
thank you, Lord, for my family.
There are many who are lonely.

Even though our breakfast table never
looks like the pictures in magazines and
the menu is at times unbalanced,
thank you, Lord, for the food we have.
There are many who are hungry.

Even though the routine of my job often is
monotonous,
thank you, Lord,
for the opportunity to work.
There are many who have no job.

Even though I grumble and bemoan my
fate from day to day and wish my
circumstances were not so modest,
thank you, Lord, for life!

Author Unknown

T39

We thank thee then, O Father,
for all things bright and good;
the seed time and the harvest;
our life, our health, our food.
Accept the gifts we offer
for all thy love imparts,
and what thou most desirest,
our humble, thankful hearts.

We Plough the Fields and Scatter Matthias Claudius

T40

All our discontents about what we want appeared to me to spring from the want of thankfulness for what we have.

Robinson Crusoe Daniel Defoe

T41

. . . Some believers came to me and told me that you are faithful to the truth. They told me that you continue to live by it. That gave me great joy. I have no greater joy than to hear that my children are living by the truth.

3 John 3,4 NIRV

T42

Seeing our Father in everything makes life one long thanksgiving and gives a rest of heart.

The Christian's Secret of a Happy Life
Hannah Whitall Smith

T43

I am so glad that you do not give up on me, Lord, but like a loving father with a small child you guide me, protect me and, when necessary, rebuke me.

T44

Friendship – such a special and precious
relationship.
We thank you so much, Father, for
our friendships; those that have lasted
many decades, those that were short-lived
but helpful and supportive at the time
and those that are only just beginning
to blossom.
Thank you for friendships that are easy,
joy-filled and comfortable; friendships
where we are able to share on the deepest
level our hopes and worries; friendships
where there is mutual respect and trust;
friendships where we can both offer and
receive loving support and counsel.
This special relationship is a great
strengthener and encourager, giving us a
sense of belonging and being loved.
For friendship, we thank you.
But most of all, Father God, we thank
you that through Jesus you said you
look on our relationship with you as
one of friendship.
How amazing is that? God is my friend.
Thank you.

Anon.

T45

Dear Heavenly Father,
I'm overwhelmed with your goodness!
You never cease to amaze me with the
surprisingly wonderful ways you
choose to bless me.

Thank you for how you filled my heart
with joy in a brand new way.
You truly are a loving Father.
But, I don't want to stop at thanking you
for the big miracles you bring into my life.
I'm just as thankful for the small things:
a baby's smile, a thoughtful gesture,
a friend's encouraging word.
And most special of all, are the unexpected
blessings you send into my life:
a brilliant sunset, a letter from an old friend,
my teenager's 'I love you'.
I praise you, Lord – the giver of blessings.

Life's Daily Prayer Book for Women
Used by permission of Thomas Nelson Gift Books

Supplication

S1

Restore, O Lord,
the honour of your name,
in works of sovereign power
come shake the earth again;
that all may see
and come with reverent fear
to the living God,
whose kingdom shall outlast the years.

Restore, O Lord Graham Kendrick and Chris Rolinson

S2

This is how you should pray:
'Our Father in heaven,
may your name be honoured.
May your kingdom come.
May what you want to happen be
  done on earth as it is done in heaven.
Give us today our daily bread.
Forgive us our sins,
just as we also have forgiven those
  who sin against us.
Keep us from falling into sin
  when we are tempted.
Save us from the evil one.'

Matthew 6:9-13 NIRV

S3

Grant us, O merciful God,
knowledge and true understanding of thy word, that we may know what thy will is, and also may show forth in our lives those things that we do know; that we be not only knowers of thy word, but also doers of the same; by our Lord and Saviour Jesus Christ.

Anon. Household of King Henry VIII

S4

Trust in the Lord with all your heart
and lean not on your own understanding;
in all your ways acknowledge him,
and he will make your paths straight.

Proverbs 3:5, 6 NIV(UK)

S5

But I tell you to love your enemies and
pray for anyone who mistreats you.

Matthew 5:44 CEV

S6

We are afflicted in every way, but not
crushed;
perplexed, but not driven to despair;
persecuted, but not forsaken;
struck down, but not destroyed.

2 Corinthians 4:8, 9 ESV

57

And the Holy Spirit helps us in our distress.

For we don't even know what we should pray for, nor how we should pray.

But the Holy Spirit prays for us with groanings that cannot be expressed in words. And the Father who knows all hearts knows what the Spirit is saying, for the Spirit pleads for us believers in harmony with God's own will.

Romans 8:26, 27 NLT

58

Beware, in your prayer, above everything, of limiting God, not only by unbelief, but by fancying that you know what he can do. Expect unexpected things, above all that we ask or think. Each time you intercede, be quiet first and worship God in his glory. Think of what he can do, of how he delights to hear Christ, of your place in Christ, and expect great things.

Helps to Intercession Andrew Murray

S9

Father, to thee I raise my whole being,
a vessel emptied of self.
Accept, Lord, this my emptiness,
and so fill me with thyself –
thy light, thy love, thy life –
that these, thy precious gifts may radiate
through me
and overflow the chalice of my heart
into the hearts of all with whom I
come in contact this day,
revealing unto them the beauty of thy joy
and wholeness
and the serenity of thy peace
which nothing can destroy.

Francis Nuttall

S10

O Breath of life,
come sweeping through us,
revive your Church with life and power.

O Breath of life,
come, cleanse, renew us
and fit your Church to meet this hour.

O Wind of God,
come bend us, break us
till humbly we confess our need;
then, in your tenderness remake us,
revive, restore – for this we plead.

O Breath of Life Elizabeth A. P. Head

S11

O God,
we pray for all those in our world who are
suffering from injustice:
for those who are discriminated against
because of their race, colour or religion;
for those imprisoned for working for the
relief of oppression;
for those who are hounded for speaking
the inconvenient truth;
for those tempted to violence as a cry
against overwhelming hardship;
for those deprived of reasonable health
and education;
for those suffering from hunger and famine;
for those too weak to help themselves
and who have no one else to help them;
for the unemployed who cry out for work
but do not find it.
We pray for anyone of our acquaintance
who is personally affected by injustice.

Forgive us, Lord, if we unwittingly share
in the conditions or in a system that
perpetuates injustice.
Show us how we can serve your children
and make your love practical by
washing their feet.

Author Unknown

S12

Lord, make me an instrument of your peace,
where there is hatred, let me sow love;
where there is injury, pardon;
where there is doubt, faith;
where there is despair, hope;
where there is darkness, light;
where there is sadness, joy;
O Divine Master, grant that I may not so
much seek to be consoled as to console;
to be understood as to understand;
to be loved as to love.
For it is in giving that we receive;
it is in pardoning that we are pardoned;
and it is in dying that we are born to
eternal life.

St Francis of Assisi

S13

Behold, Lord,
an empty vessel that needs to be filled.
My Lord, fill it.

I am weak in the faith; strengthen me.

I am cold in love;
warm me and make me fervent,
that my love might go out to my neighbour.

I do not have a strong and firm faith;
at times I doubt,
and am unable to trust you altogether.

O Lord, help me.

Martin Luther

S14

I urge, then, first of all, that requests, prayers, intercession and thanksgiving be made for everyone – for kings and all those in authority, that we may live peaceful and quiet lives in all godliness and holiness. This is good, and pleases God our Saviour, who wants all people to be saved and to come to a knowledge of the truth. For there is one God and one mediator between God and humanity, the man Christ Jesus, who gave himself as a ransom for all people – the testimony given in its proper time.

1 Timothy 2:1-6 NIV(UK)

S15

In late autumn of the twentieth year of King Artaxerxes' reign, I was at the fortress of Susa. Hanani, one of my brothers, came to visit me with some other men who had just arrived from Judah. I asked them about the Jews who had survived the captivity and about how things were going in Jerusalem. They said to me, 'Things are not going well for those who returned to the province of Judah. They are in great trouble and disgrace. The wall of Jerusalem has been torn down, and the gates have been burned.'

When I heard this, I sat down and wept. In fact, for days I mourned, fasted, and prayed to the God of heaven. Then I said, 'O Lord, God of heaven, the great and awesome God who keeps his covenant of unfailing love with those who love him and obey his commands, listen to my prayer! Look down and see me praying night and day for your people Israel.'

Nehemiah 1:1-6a NLT

S16

I'm so very ordinary,
nothing special on my own.
I have never walked on water,
I have never calmed a storm.
Sometimes I'm hiding away
from the madness around me,
like a child who's afraid of the dark,
but when I call on Jesus,
all things are possible.
I can mount on wings like eagles and soar.
When I call on Jesus,
mountains are gonna fall
cause he'll move heaven and earth
to come rescue me when I call.

Call On Jesus Nicole C. Mullen

S17

We beseech thee, Master,
to be our helper and protector.
Save the afflicted among us;
have mercy on the lowly;
raise up the fallen;
appear to the needy;
heal the ungodly;
restore the wanderers of thy people;
feed the hungry;
ransom our prisoners;
raise up the sick;
comfort the faint-hearted.

Pope Clement I

S18

Then Jonah prayed to the Lord his God while in the stomach of the fish, saying, 'I called out to the Lord because of my trouble, and he answered me. I cried for help from the place of the dead, and you heard my voice. You threw me into the deep waters, to the very bottom of the sea. A flood was all around me and all your waves passed over me. Then I said, "I have been sent away from your eyes. But I will look again toward your holy house." Waters closed in over me. The sea was all around me. Weeds were around my head. I went down to the roots of the mountains. The walls of the earth were around me forever. But you have brought me up from the grave, O Lord my God. While I was losing all my strength, I remembered the Lord. And my prayer came to you, into your holy house. Those who worship false Gods have given up their faith in you. But I will give gifts in worship to you with a thankful voice. I will give you what I have promised. The Lord is the one who saves.' Then the Lord spoke to the fish, and it spit Jonah out onto the dry land.

Jonah 2 NLV

S19

O thou God of all beings, of all worlds,
and of all times,
we pray that the little differences in
our clothes,
in our inadequate languages,
in our ridiculous customs,
in our imperfect laws,
in our illogical opinions,
in our ranks and conditions
which are so disproportionately
important to us
and so meaningless to you,
that these small variations that distinguish
those atoms that we call humankind,
one from another,
may not be signals of hatred and
persecution!

Voltaire

S20

Take my life, and let it be
consecrated, Lord, to thee;
take my moments and my days,
let them flow in ceaseless praise.

Take my will, and make it thine;
it shall be no longer mine;
take my heart, it is thine own;
it shall be thy royal throne.

Take my love; my Lord, I pour
at thy feet its treasure store;
take myself, and I will be
ever, only, all for thee.

Take My Life and Let It Be Frances Ridley Havergal

S21

Watch, O Lord, with those who wake,
or watch, or weep tonight, and give your
angels charge over those who sleep.

Tend your sick ones, O Lord Christ.
Rest your weary ones.
Bless your dying ones.
Soothe your suffering ones.
Pity your afflicted ones.
Shield your joyous ones.
And all for your love's sake.

Amen.

St Augustine of Hippo

S22

Against the persecution of a tyrant the godly have no remedy but prayer.

John Calvin

S23

During the time Jesus lived on earth, he prayed and asked God with loud cries and tears. Jesus' prayer was to God who was able to save him from death. God heard Christ because Christ honoured God.

Hebrews 5:7 NLV

S24

Remember the Lord's people who are in
jail and be concerned for them.

Don't forget those who are suffering,
but imagine that you are there with them.

Hebrews 13:3 CEV

S25

Our divisions prevent our neighbours from hearing the gospel as they should.

Pope John Paul II

S26

All praise to the God and Father of our
Master, Jesus the Messiah!
Father of all mercy!
God of all healing counsel!
He comes alongside us when we go
through hard times, and before you know
it, he brings us alongside someone else
who is going through hard times so that
we can be there for that person just as God
was there for us. We have plenty of hard
times that come from following the
Messiah, but no more so than the good
times of his healing comfort –
we get a full measure of that, too.

2 Corinthians 1:3-5 TM

S27

I sit on a man's back, choking him and making him carry me, and yet assure myself and others that I am very sorry for him and wish to ease his lot by all possible means – except by getting off his back.

S28

If any of you lacks wisdom, he should ask God, who gives generously to all without finding fault, and it will be given to him. But when he asks, he must believe and not doubt, because he who doubts is like a wave of the sea, blown and tossed by the wind.

James 1:5,6 NIV(UK)

S29

Lord of all hopefulness,
Lord of all joy,
whose trust, ever child-like,
no cares could destroy;
be there at our waking,
and give us, we pray,
your bliss in our hearts, Lord,
at the break of the day.

Lord of all eagerness,
Lord of all faith,
whose strong hands were skilled
at the plane and the lathe;
be there at our labours,
and give us, we pray,
your strength in our hearts, Lord,
at the noon of the day.

Lord of all kindliness,
Lord of all grace,
your hands swift to welcome,
your arms to embrace;
be there at our homing,
and give us, we pray,
your love in our hearts, Lord,
at the eve of the day.

Lord of all gentleness,
Lord of all calm,
whose voice is contentment,
whose presence is balm;
be there at our sleeping,
and give us, we pray,
your peace in our hearts, Lord,
at the end of the day.

Lord of All Hopefulness Jan Struther

S30

O God of many names,
lover of all nations,
we pray for peace in our hearts,
in our homes, in our nations, in our world,
the peace of your will,
the peace of our need.

Bishop George Appleton

S31

Father, I place into your hands . . .

. . . the things I cannot do.

. . . the times that I've been through.

. . . the way that I should go,

. . . my friends and my family.

. . . the things that trouble me.

. . . the person I would be,

for I know I always can trust you.

Father, I Place into Your Hands Jenny Hewer

S32

Take, Lord, all my liberty.
Receive my memory,
my understanding,
and my whole will.

Whatever I have and possess,
you have given me;
to you I restore it wholly,
and to your will I utterly surrender it
for my direction.

Give me the love of you only,
with your grace,
and I am rich enough;
nor do I ask anything besides.

St Ignatius of Loyola

S33

Depend on it.

God's work, done in God's way,
will never lack God's supply.

He is too wise a God to frustrate his
purposes for lack of funds,
and he can just as easily supply them
ahead of time as afterwards,
and he much prefers doing so.

J. Hudson Taylor

S34

Have mercy on me, O Lord, for I call to
you all day long.
Bring joy to your servant, for to you,
O Lord, I lift up my soul.
You are forgiving and good, O Lord,
abounding in love to all who call to you.
Hear my prayer, O Lord; listen to my cry
for mercy.
In the day of my trouble I will call to you,
for you will answer me.
Among the gods there is none like you,
O Lord; no deeds can compare with yours.
All the nations you have made will come
and worship before you, O Lord;
they will bring glory to your name.
For you are great and do marvellous
deeds; you alone are God.
Teach me your way, O Lord, and I will
walk in your truth;
give me an undivided heart, that I may
fear your name.
I will praise you, O Lord my God, with all
my heart; I will glorify your name forever.

Psalm 86:3-12 NIV(UK)

S35

Dear Lord,
I may not see the sun and moon lose their light. I may not witness rivers turn red, or stars fall from the sky. Yet there are times when my world becomes unhinged and the foundations of what I believe crack and dissolve.

Give me the grace to believe that your power is at work in the turmoil of my life. Lead me to remember that your power is greater than all evil, and though the world may rock and sometimes break, it will in time be transformed by your love.

Author Unknown

S36

Violence never again!
War never again!
Terrorism never again!

In God's name,
may all religions bring upon earth
justice and peace, forgiveness, life and love!

Pope John Paul II

S37

Should we feel at times disheartened and discouraged, a confiding thought, a simple movement of heart towards God will renew our powers.

Whatever he may demand of us, he will give us at the moment the strength and the courage that we need.

François de Salignac de la Mothe-Fénelon

S38

These things I have spoken to you while
being present with you.

But the helper, the Holy Spirit,
whom the Father will send in my name,
he will teach you all things,
and bring to your remembrance
all things that I said to you.

Peace I leave with you,
my peace I give to you;
not as the world gives do I give to you.
Let not your heart be troubled,
neither let it be afraid.

John 14:25-27 NKJV

S39

Disturb us, Lord, when we are too well-pleased with ourselves, when our dreams have come true because we have dreamed too little, when we arrived safely because we sailed too close to the shore.

Disturb us, Lord, when, with the abundance of things we possess, we have lost our thirst for the waters of life; having fallen in love with life, we have ceased to dream of eternity and in our efforts to build a new earth, we have allowed our vision of the new heaven to dim.

Disturb us, Lord, to dare more boldly to venture on wider seas where storms will show your mastery; where losing sight of land, we shall find the stars.
We ask you to push back the horizons of our hopes; and to push us into the future in strength, courage, hope, and love.

Attributed to Sir Francis Drake

S40

I shall pass through this world but once. Any good thing therefore that I can do, or any kindness that I can show to any human being, let me do it now. Let me not defer it or neglect it, for I shall not pass this way again.

Henry Drummond

S41

When the world loses its lustre,
and you're feeling sad and lonely,
and you need someone to be there
in your time of need;
you can turn your eyes to the heavens,
and their Creator's watching over you
with arms of love to hold you,
and draw you near.
Don't worry, no matter,
he hears you, keep praying.

Draw You Near Lisa Kimmey Bragg

S42

This is God's word on the subject:
'I know what I'm doing.
I have it all planned out – plans to take care of you, not abandon you, plans to give you the future you hope for. When you call on me, when you come and pray to me, I'll listen. When you come looking for me, you'll find me. Yes, when you get serious about finding me and want it more than anything else, I'll make sure you won't be disappointed.'

Jeremiah 29:11-13 TM

S43

Now I say to you in conclusion, life is hard, at times as hard as crucible steel. It has its bleak and difficult moments. Like the ever-flowing waters of the river, life has its moments of drought and its moments of flood. Like the ever-changing cycle of the seasons, life has the soothing warmth of its summers and the piercing chill of its winters. But if one will hold on, he will discover that God walks with him, and that God is able to lift you from the fatigue of despair to the buoyancy of hope and transform dark and desolate valleys into sunlit paths of inner peace.

Martin Luther King

S44

My God, I believe most firmly that you watch over all who hope in you, and that we can want for nothing when we rely upon you in all things. Therefore, I am resolved for the future to cast all my cares upon you.

St Claude de la Colombière

S45

Be persevering in your prayers and be thankful as you stay awake to pray.

Pray for us especially, asking God to throw open a door for us to announce the message and proclaim the mystery of Christ, for the sake of which I am in chains.

Pray that I may proclaim it as clearly as I ought.

Colossians 4:2-4 NJB

Sources

Adoration Sources

A1 *Genesis 1:31a KJV.*

A2 C. S. Lewis, *The Problem of Pain* (1940).

A3 *Exodus 3:14 NIV(UK).*

A4 *Isaiah 40:25 NLT.*

A5 Judy Horner-Montemayor, *'Who Is Like Unto Thee', Songs of Fellowship Volume 1* (1975).

A6 *Traditional Ethiopian Jewish Prayer,* translated by Margaret Hayon.

A7 *Psalm 102:25-27 NKJV.*

A8 Jonathan Edwards.

A9 Ruth Dryden, *'Within the Veil'* (1978).

A10 Andy Bromley and Chris Donohue, *'Clothed with Splendour', Beautiful River,* Grapevine 2002 (1999).

A11 *Psalm 76:4,7a NRSV.*

A12 St Francis of Assisi.

A13 *Revelation 15:2b-4 NLT.*

A14 Thomas John Watson.

A15 *1 Chronicles 29:10, 11 NIV(UK).*

A16 Frederick W. Faber, *'There's a Wideness in God's Mercy'* (1854).

A17 Tim Hughes, *'Beautiful One', When Silence Falls* (2002).

A18 *Romans 11:33-36 NJB.*

A19 J. S. B. Monsell, *'O Worship the Lord'* (1863).

A20 *Job 11:7-9 CEV.*

A21 *Psalm 108:3-5 NIV(UK).*

A22 John Bunyan, *The Pilgrim's Progress* (1678).

A23 Mary Kirkbride-Barthow and Mary Lou King, '*Ascribe Greatness*' (1979).
A24 *Jeremiah 10:7 NJB.*
A25 *Psalm 36:5,6 NLT.*
A26 A. W. Tozer, *The Pursuit of God* (Christian Publications, 1982).
A27 *Revelation 4:8b JB.*
A28 Frederick W. Faber, '*My God, How Wonderful You Are*' (1849).
A29 *Jewish Evening Prayer.*
A30 Anon.
A31 *Job 9:8-10 NIV(UK).*
A32 Malcolm du Plessis, '*We Declare Your Majesty*' (1984).
A33 Nick Fawcett, *Daily Prayer Time With God* (Kevin Mayhew Ltd, 2003).
A34 *After St James.*
A35 *Psalm 8:1 NIV(UK).*
A36 *Psalm 93 CEV.*
A37 Timothy Dudley-Smith, '*Timeless Love! We Sing the Story*'.
A38 *Ecclesiastes 3:11 NLV.*
A39 *Adapted from a Jewish Morning Prayer.*
A40 *Lamentations 3:22, 23 ESV.*
A41 John Birch.
A42 *Isaiah 25:1 NIV(UK).*
A43 *Jeremiah 23:23, 24 NIV(UK).*
A44 Dietrich Bonhoeffer.
A45 Dave Bilbrough, '*This Is the Place*' (1997).

Confession Sources

C1 *Colossians 1:21-23 TM.*
C2 *Galatians 6:8 NLV.*
C3 John G. Whittier, *'Dear Lord and Father of Mankind'* (1872).
C4 *Prayers from the Heart: Simple Conversations With God* (Honor Books, 1999).
C5 *Job 11:13-15 TYB.*
C6 Charles H. Spurgeon.
C7 Freda Lindsay, *'At the Foot of the Cross'*.
C8 Graham Kendrick, *'We Worship at Your Feet'* (1989).
C9 *Luke 5:32 NRSV.*
C10 *Life's Daily Prayer Book for Women* (Thomas Nelson, 2004).
C11 *Isaiah 44:22, 23 NLT.*
C12 William Shakespeare, *Hamlet* (1624).
C13 *James 4:8 TM.*
C14 Augustus Montague Toplady, *'Rock of Ages'* (1776).
C15 Paul Landers, *'I Kneel'*.
C16 *1 Peter 2:1-3 NIRV.*
C17 *Psalm 103:8-12 TM.*
C18 Maud Battersby, *An Evening Prayer* (1911).
C19 Susan Howatch, *A Question of Integrity* (Time Warner, 1998).
C20 Martin Luther.
C21 Chris Bowater, *'God of Grace'*, *Time for Tears* (2005).

C22 *Proverbs 20:9 RSV.*
C23 Dave Bilbrough, *'I'm On My Knees', Personal Worship 2* (2000).
C24 *A General Confession, Book of Common Prayer* (1662). Crown copyright, reproduced by permission.
C25 *Proverbs 28:13 NLT.*
C26 Anon.
C27 *1Timothy 1:12-16 ESV.*
C28 Charitie L. Bancroft, *'Before the Throne of God Above'* (1863).
C29 *Ephesians 4:20-32 TM.*
C30 *Ecclesiastes 7:20 NIV(UK).*
C31 Bishop Thomas Wilson.
C32 *Psalm 32:5 JB.*
C33 Dougie Brown, *'River Wash Over Me'* (1980).
C34 *Ezekiel 18:30b, 31 NIRV.*
C35 Oscar Wilde, *De Profundis* (1897).
C36 Frederick W. Faber, *'I Am Trusting Thee, Lord Jesus'*.
C37 *Matthew 3:2 TYB.*
C38 Edwin Hatch, *'Breathe on Me, Breath of God'* (1878).
C39 *Ephesians 2:4-10 NLV.*
C40 Carl Frederick Buechner.
C41 *Isaiah 1:18 KJV.*
C42 Revd Bill McGinnis.
C43 Charlotte Elliot, *'Just as I Am'* (1835).
C44 *Micah 7:18, 19 NIV(UK).*
C45 *1 John 1:8, 9 JB.*

Thanksgiving Sources

T1 Mark Altrogge, *'I'm Forever Grateful'* (1986).

T2 *Revelation 7:11, 12 WWE(NT).*

T3 Nick Fawcett, *Prayers for All Seasons Book Two* (Kevin Mayhew Ltd, 2001).

T4 Dave Bilbrough, *'I Am a New Creation'* (1983).

T5 Vicky Beeching, *'The Greatest Gift', New Songs 2003/2004 Vol. 1* (2002).

T6 *1 Thessalonians 5:16-18 NIV(UK).*

T7 Warren D. Cornell, *'Wonderful Peace'* (1889).

T8 Albert Schweitzer.

T9 William Shakespeare, *King Henry VI (Part I)* (1587).

T10 *2 Thessalonians 1:3 NLT.*

T11 Noel Richards, *'You Laid Aside Your Majesty'* (1985).

T12 *Luke 9:16 NLV.*

T13 Stuart K. Hine, *'O Lord, My God!'* (1953).

T14 *Ezra 3:10-12 CEV.*

T15 Joni Eareckson Tada.

T16 *Psalm 50:14 NRSV.*

T17 Nancy Parker Brummett, *Simply the Savior* (Cook Communications Ministries, 1998).

T18 Ralph Waldo Emerson.

T19 *Isaiah 12:4-6 NIV(UK).*

T20 Matt Redman, *'Rejoice With Trembling'* (2002).

T21 *The Australian Prayer Book* (1978).
T22 *1 Peter 1:3-7 TM.*
T23 *Luke 1:46-55 NLV.*
T24 Ainsley Carry.
T25 *Luke 17:11-19 WWE(NT).*
T26 John Newton, *'Amazing Grace'* (1772).
T27 Matt Redman, *'Once Again'* (1995).
T28 *Philippians 4:12-14 TYB.*
T29 *Habakkuk 3:17-19 NIRV.*
T30 *Traditional Mealtime Blessing.*
T31 Walter Rauschenbusch.
T32 Ralph Waldo Emerson.
T33 *2 Corinthians 2:14 NKJV.*
T34 Revd Bill McGinnis.
T35 William Rees, *'Here is Love, Vast as the Ocean'* (trans. William Edwards, 1900).
T36 Timothy Dudley-Smith, *'Tell Out My Soul'* (1962).
T37 *Colossians 3:15-17 ESV.*
T38 Author Unknown.
T39 Matthias Claudius, *'We Plough the Fields and Scatter'* (1782).
T40 Daniel Defoe, *Robinson Crusoe* (1719).
T41 *3 John 3, 4 NIRV.*
T42 Hannah Whitall Smith, *The Christian's Secret of a Happy Life* (Whitaker House, 1983).
T43 Ian Coffey with Kim Bush, *Windows on the World from the Word*, (BRF, 2001).
T44 Anon.
T45 *Life's Daily Prayer Book for Women* (Thomas Nelson, 2004).

Supplication Sources

S1 Graham Kendrick and Chris Rolinson, '*Restore, O Lord*' (1981).
S2 *Matthew 6:9-13 NIRV.*
S3 Anon, Household of King Henry VIII.
S4 *Proverbs 3:5, 6 NIV(UK).*
S5 *Matthew 5:44 CEV.*
S6 *2 Corinthians 4:8, 9 ESV.*
S7 *Romans 8:26, 27 NLT.*
S8 Andrew Murray, *Helps to Intercession* (Christian Literature Crusade, 2001).
S9 Francis Nuttall.
S10 Elizabeth A. P. Head, '*O Breath of Life*' (1914).
S11 Author Unknown.
S12 St Francis of Assisi.
S13 Martin Luther.
S14 *1 Timothy 2:1-6 NIV(UK).*
S15 *Nehemiah 1:1-6a NLT.*
S16 Nicole C. Mullen, '*Call On Jesus*' (2001).
S17 Pope Clement I.
S18 *Jonah 2 NLV.*
S19 Voltaire.
S20 Frances Ridley Havergal, '*Take My Life and Let It Be*' (1874).
S21 St Augustine of Hippo.
S22 John Calvin.
S23 *Hebrews 5:7 NLV.*
S24 *Hebrews 13:3 CEV.*
S25 Pope John Paul II.
S26 *2 Corinthians 1:3-5 TM.*

S27 Leo Tolstoy, *Writings on Civil Disobedience and Nonviolence* (New Society Publishers, 1987).

S28 *James 1:5, 6 NIV(UK).*

S29 Jan Struther, *'Lord of All Hopefulness', in Enlarged Songs of Praise* (Oxford University Press, 1931).

S30 Bishop George Appleton.

S31 Jenny Hewer, *'Father, I Place into Your Hands'* (1975).

S32 St Ignatius of Loyola.

S33 J. Hudson Taylor.

S34 *Psalm 86:3-12 NIV(UK).*

S35 Author Unknown.

S36 Pope John Paul II.

S37 François de Salignac de la Mothe-Fénelon.

S38 *John 14:25-27 NKJV.*

S39 Attributed to Sir Francis Drake.

S40 Henry Drummond.

S41 Lisa Kimmey Bragg, *'Draw You Near', No Turning Back* (1999).

S42 *Jeremiah 29:11-13 TM.*

S43 Martin Luther King.

S44 St Claude de la Colombière.

S45 *Colossians 4:2-4 NJB.*

Part Three
REFERENCE MATERIAL

At a Glance

Mark Altrogge is Senior Pastor of Lord of Life Church in Indiana, Pennsylvania. He is a firm believer in memorising scripture in order to apply it to everyday life, counselling and witnessing. He found that putting scripture to music helped people to memorise it more easily. The song *I'm Forever Grateful* demonstrates Mark's desire to create a worship song that combined an emotional melody with theological messages. His website is www.forevergratefulmusic.com. (p. 141)

Bishop George Appleton (1902-93), born a gardener's son, grew up to lead an active and varied ministry in the Anglican Church. His ministry included serving as Archdeacon of London, Canon of St Paul's Cathedral, Archbishop of Perth, Australia and Bishop of Jerusalem. He is well known for his spiritual writings on prayer and meditation and had a regular column in the Daily Telegraph. Bishop Appleton compiled a collection of over 1,000 prayers from across centuries and traditions, including Christian, Jewish, Muslim, Hindu, Buddhist, Shinto, native American and Bahá'í. (p. 219)

St Augustine of Hippo (354-430) was born to a Christian mother, though he himself led a wild life trying many different religions and philosophies. After reading St Paul's letters, he finally committed himself to Christ at the age of 33 and was ordained priest in his native North Africa. As a preacher he was well known for his encouragement not just during his own lifetime, but down the ages and even today. Augustine understood the inward struggles that people had and his honesty and frankness were always appreciated. His collection of autobiographical books, *Confessions,* contains some very powerful words and prayers. (p. 209)

Charitie L. Bancroft (1841-1923) was born into a clergy family in County Dublin, Ireland. She wrote lots of hymns that were published in Lyra Britannica (a collection of British hymns), in Bishop Ryle's Spiritual Songs (used at cottage meetings) and even on leaflets. The hymn for which she is best remembered, *Before the Throne of God Above,* was written in 1863 and has been popularised by the tune composed in 1997 by Vikki Cook. (p. 118)

Vicky Beeching has been writing worship songs for more than ten years after leading the worship group at her church as a teenager. She first gained recognition for her song writing ability while at Oxford University, where she studied theology. The song *The Greatest Gift,* is on the album New Songs 2003/2004 Vol. 1. Vicky's website is www.vickybeeching.com. (p. 145)

Dave Bilbrough is widely recognised as one of the UK's best known worship leaders and songwriters. After committing himself to Christ in 1971, Dave aimed to make worship more meaningful for young Christians who, like himself, were struggling to understand and make use of many of the dated hymns. He now takes teams of young musicians to Third World countries, not only to give fundraising concerts that support mission work, but also to encourage, train and support musicians there. Dave received two Gold awards from the Christian Broadcasting Council Annual Media Awards in 2005. *This is My Worship* was named Best Christian Music DVD, whilst his Tsunami Benefit concert shown worldwide on God TV was awarded Best Christian Music TV Programme. The song

I'm On My Knees is taken from his *Personal Worship 2* album, released in 2000. Dave has also written three books demonstrating how to ground worship in themes of grace, mission and the presence of God. Dave's website is www.davebilbrough.com. (pp. 28, 87, 113 and 144)

John Birch, a Methodist lay preacher and worship leader living in Wales, is a contributor to the International Bible Reading Fellowship notes. He is passionate about his country's Christian heritage and his prayers reflect his desire for the world to think about and dwell on the magnificence of creation in order to fully reflect awe and wonder in prayer. His prayer book entitled *heart2heart* encourages this sense of adoration. His prayers have also appeared on the Christian Aid website, Baptist Resources and other publications. His website is www.faithandworship.com. (p. 83)

Dietrich Bonhoeffer (1906-45) was a theologian, spiritual writer and author of fiction and poetry. His leadership in the anti-Nazi Confessing Church made him an advocate of the Jews. After helping a group of Jews escape to Switzerland, he was arrested and imprisoned in 1943. Bonhoeffer was one of four members of his immediate family to die during the Nazi regime as a result of their participation in the small Protestant resistance movement. He was hanged in the concentration camp at Flossenbürg on 9 April, 1945. The letters he wrote during these final two years of his life were posthumously published as *Letters and Papers from Prison* and *Love Letters from Cell 92*. (p. 86)

Chris Bowater has been involved in pioneering worship conferences all over the world, as well as giving his time to national conferences like Spring Harvest, Kingdom Faith and Life in the Spirit. His songs are featured on many albums, including *Time for Tears 2005,* from which the song *God of Grace* is taken. His website is www.chrisbowater.com. (p. 111)

Andy Bromley is a worship leader and singer/songwriter who has been leading worship since he was 15 years old. At the age of 22 he became Worship Pastor for King's Community Church in Bedworth, where he has been based for the last 16 years. Andy has also been leading worship at Christian events since 1999, including Songs of Praise, Spring Harvest and Grapevine. The album *Beautiful River, Grapevine 2002,* from which the song *Clothed in Splendour* is taken, marks 22 years of the Grapevine event, an inter-church, multi-network event in Lincolnshire that celebrates the Christian message in a variety of ways. (pp. 20 and 52)

Nancy Parker Brummett is a freelance writer living in Colorado Springs. She wrote the book *Simply the Savior* to help other women to live a simplified life in Christ. By looking at life from Christ's perspective and living with the Holy Spirit, Nancy writes that women can prioritise their actions and make decisions in all aspects of their lives without feelings of guilt. (p. 157)

Carl Frederick Buechner was an English teacher and novelist before converting to Christianity in 1953 and being ordained as an evangelist in 1958. Although his official title was 'evangelist', he preferred to think of himself as an 'apologist', stating that his job was to present the faith as appealingly, honestly, relevantly and skilfully as possible. (p. 132)

John Bunyan (1628-88) was born the son of a tinker yet was able to have some education through the connections of his slightly higher-born mother. After the English Civil War, he began attending a new religious congregation meeting in Bedford. Following the death of the pastor, Bunyan took over his role as head of the congregation and began life as a travelling preacher. After the Restoration of the monarchy in 1660, preaching was forbidden, in an attempt to restrain the growth of independent congregations. When Bunyan refused to stop preaching, he was arrested, tried and held in the county jail until he agreed to conform.

He remained in jail for the next 12 years and although conditions were poor he was allowed visitors and was even allowed out occasionally for the day. He spent his time writing a number of books on religious themes, including his biography. In 1672 when Charles II issued his Declaration of Religious Indulgences, Bunyan was released. He bought a barn and converted it to a home for his independent congregation. In 1673 however, the king repealed his Declaration and Bunyan was sent back into jail. It is probable that it was during this imprisonment that he wrote the religious allegorical novel, *The Pilgrim's Progress*. (p. 64)

Kim Bush has been involved with a number of ventures, including running her own desktop publishing business and working alongside her husband Jon, a Baptist minister in churches in the UK and USA. In addition, she has raised three children, worked in a doctor's surgery and more recently has started a course of study in English literature with philosophy. Taking a selection of articles from the Ian Coffey Column published in the Western Morning News, she added Bible passages, reflections and short prayers which over the past three years have resulted in three published books. (p. 184)

John Calvin (1509-64), born in France, studied theology at the University of Paris despite pressure by his father to study law. When his father's death released him from such pressures Calvin pursued his religious vocation, embracing humanistic leanings before suddenly converting to Protestantism. He became very critical of abuses in the French Catholic Church, strongly believing that God had chosen him to create a spiritual renewal in the world. His ideas were considered heretical: he believed that man was born corrupt to face an omnipotent God who had, before the world was created, pre-destined some (the Elect) to be saved through his grace, and some (the Reprobate) to suffer eternal damnation. A Reprobate could never claim divine grace but could only ever achieve an inner conviction of salvation, while an Elect could never fall from grace, whatever he did. Calvin also preached that people could only approach God through faith in Christ – not through Mass and pilgrimages. He claimed that the New Testament, baptism and the Eucharist had been created to provide humanity with continual divine guidance when seeking faith. Branded as a heretic, Calvin fled a Paris that in the following year saw 24 heretics burned at the stake.

In 1536 he published *Institutes of the Christian Religion*, a book that explained his religious beliefs and detailed how his church should be organised. His services were plain, with an emphasis on logical and learned sermons. Despite a love of music, he did not believe that it held a valid place in religious services, claiming that it acted as a distraction. Although instruments were banned, congregational singing was allowed, usually in the form of psalms. (p. 210)

Ainsley Carry is an American Christian currently working as Assistant Vice President of Student Affairs at the University of Florida. He is a strong advocate for student leadership and personal development, believing that the central mission of higher education is to develop competent leaders. (p. 164)

Matthias Claudius (1740-1815) was a German poet and writer. He studied law and languages at university, after switching from theology due to ill health and a lack of commitment to the subject. A growing interest in literature led him away from his studies and he returned home without completing them. Working as secretary to an advisor of the Danish crown, Claudius began to move in literary circles. His interest led to work in editing but realising that his income would not support a wife and family, he collected for publication all his fictional letters, verses, reviews of recently published books and criticism on topics such as philosophy, music and politics. Even so, this was still insufficient to supplement his income. A bout of pleurisy led to deteriorating health and after the Napoleonic Wars forced him and his wife to move from place to place for a year, he never fully regained his health. (p. 180)

Pope Clement I (d. circa AD 101) is generally thought to be the first successor to St Peter as bishop of Rome. There is discrepancy about his life and death, with myth and fact interwoven. Tertullian, writing in about AD 199, claimed that Clement was ordained by St Peter himself but dating errors by the early writers make this unlikely. What does seem to be in agreement, however, is that he was the writer of an *Epistle to the Corinthians,* (not to be confused with the letter in the Bible) dated around AD 96 in the last year of the Roman Emperor Domitian. The epistle, still preserved today, does not actually mention his name, but is alluded to in a different letter, one from Corinth to Rome a few decades later, in which the writer says 'the letter we received from your bishop Clement, which we still read regularly'. Legend has it that Clement died a martyr's death at the hands of Domitian, by being tied to an anchor and thrown into the sea but confusion over dates makes it more likely that his death, however it occurred, was in the reign of the following Emperor, Trajan. (p. 205)

Ian Coffey has been in Christian ministry for over 30 years, leading churches and mission organisations. He is currently senior minister of Crossroads Church, Geneva. While in ministry in Plymouth at a Baptist church, he wrote a weekly column for the Western Morning News, giving a Christian perspective on topical events. His articles along with Kim Bush's reflective additions have produced the *Windows on the World* books. He is currently on the leadership team of Spring Harvest. (p. 184)

St Claude de la Colombière (1641-82) was a French Jesuit who preached against Jansenism, advocating dedication to the Sacred Heart of Jesus. Whilst acting as the chaplain to the Duchess of York, he converted many Protestants through the example of his holy life. Colombière was imprisoned on suspicion of being part of a Popish plot against the king. It was only by the efforts of Louis XIV, who had recommended him for the post, that he was not martyred. With his health ruined from his prison ordeal, Colombière was banished from England and returned to France to die. He was beatified in 1929 by Pope Pius XI and canonised in 1992 by Pope John Paul II. (p. 233)

Warren D. Cornell (1858-1901) was a poet, evangelist, and preacher. In 1889, while at a Methodist camp meeting in Wisconsin, he inadvertently dropped the paper on which he had been writing his thoughts. Later, the song leader W. George Cooper found the words, made some alterations and composed a tune, so completing the hymn we know as *Wonderful Peace.* (p. 147)

Daniel Defoe (1660-1731) was born in London in 1660 and, with the intention of becoming a minister, attended Morton's Academy, a school for dissenters at Newington Green. Amongst other things, dissenters opposed state interference in religious matters. After changing his mind he became a hosiery merchant instead. Defoe became popular with King William III, after the publication of his poem *The True Born Englishman* in which he attacked people who were prejudiced against having a king of foreign birth. Having upset some very powerful people with his satirical writing, *The Shortest Way with the Dissenters,* he then spent time in Newgate. In 1703 a Tory government official employed Defoe as a spy; realising how Defoe's skill in writing could be used to mould public opinion, he instructed him to write reports on political and social issues for *The Review.* In 1719 Defoe began writing novels, including his best-known books *Robinson Crusoe* and *Moll Flanders*. His prolific publication of hundreds of books and pamphlets gained him recognition as the founder of British journalism. (p. 181)

Sir Francis Drake (c.1540-96) was an English privateer, navigator, slave trader, politician, civil engineer and vice admiral in command of the English fleet during the Elizabethan era. He is most famous for his circumnavigation of the world and for his defeat of the Spanish Armada. Drake died of dysentery after an unsuccessful attack on San Juan, Puerto Rico in 1596. He was buried at sea, in a lead coffin. (p. 228)

Henry Drummond (1851-97) was an ordained minister whose commitment to Christ began at an early age. When Dwight L. Moody visited Britain in 1873 as part of his great evangelical mission, Drummond interrupted his studies in divinity to work with him. After completing his studies, Drummond applied for a lecturing post in Natural Science at the Free Church College, Glasgow, a post that would allow him to combine his passion for both science and evangelism. He was accepted in the post, was ordained and gave his first lecture on the subject of *The Contribution of Science to Christianity*. Keen to challenge the doubts raised by Charles Darwin's *Origin of Species,* Drummond maintained that science and religion were united in revealing God to humanity. Drummond's best-known book *The Greatest Thing in the World* was based on a talk that he had given highlighting the importance of the message of love in 1 Corinthians 13. (p. 229)

Timothy Dudley-Smith was born in 1926 in Manchester and ordained a priest in 1951. He served in the Diocese of Norwich for 20 years, first as Archdeacon of Norwich, and then as Bishop of Thetford. Timothy has published about 300 hymn texts. In 1997, he achieved the rare honour for a British hymn writer of being named a 'Fellow' in the Hymn Society of the United States and Canada. His website is www.timothydudley-smith.com. (pp. 79 and 176)

Joni Eareckson Tada founded Joni and Friends, a Christian organisation that focuses on ministry in the disabled community. Joni became a quadriplegic after a diving accident in 1967. After learning to paint with a brush between her teeth, she was encouraged when a local television programme highlighted her work. Such exposure led to the Billy Graham film ministry doing a story on her life, prompting Joni to respond to the thousands of letters from disabled people by beginning her important ministry. Joni has written over 30 books and has been awarded several honours for her courage and her work. More information on Joni and her ministry can be found at www.joniandfriends.org. (p. 155)

Jonathan Edwards (1703-58) was a Puritan born into an evangelical home. In 1726, he became pastor of the largest and most influential church in Northampton, Massachusetts. In the First Great Awakening during the 1730s and 1740s, he became an internationally renowned revivalist preacher. In 1750 he was dismissed from his church after he tried to insist on stricter qualifications for admission to the sacraments. He moved on to pastor a small English congregation in another part of Massachusetts while at the same time being missionary to several Native American families from the Mohawk and Mohican tribes. His challenging and thoughtful writings have been debated for well over a century. His hopes of writing two treatises, one showing the link between the Old and New Testaments and the other on Redemption, were never realised because he died from complications from a smallpox vaccination before he could complete them. (p. 50)

Charlotte Elliot (1789-1871) suffered a serious illness at the age of 32, leaving her an invalid for the rest of her life. Her declining ill health caused her distress and when she confided to Henri Malan, a visiting Swiss preacher and evangelist, that she did not know how to find Christ, Malan's reply was, 'Come to him just as you are.' Charlotte owed her conversion to this reply and in 1835 she wrote *Just as I Am,* a hymn that reflected her humble understanding of her soul. The hymn was used to raise funds to build a school for poor pastors' daughters, raising more money than all the other fundraising projects combined. (p. 135)

Ralph Waldo Emerson (1803-82) was a Unitarian minister who left the ministry to pursue a career in philosophical writing and public speaking. He continued to preach sporadically but after a dispute with the Unitarian church he was branded a heretic, leading to a period of self-reflection. Emerson became an enthusiastic advocate of free expression, committing himself to full-time writing of new ideas. (pp. 158 and 172)

Frederick W. Faber (1814-63), born in Yorkshire, was originally an Anglican clergyman before converting to become a Roman Catholic priest. Distancing himself from his

Anglican past he highlighted the differences between the two approaches by displaying the extravagance that he associated with Roman Catholicism. He founded the London Oratory in 1848. (pp. 58, 70 and 127)

Nick Fawcett overcame a speech impediment to pursue his vocation as a Baptist minister. He served as a chaplain with the national charity *Toc H*. His difficulties with the spoken word steered him towards discovering a gift for mission through the written word and his books have reached a much greater audience than pastoral ministry would have allowed. In addition to his writing, Nick works for a variety of publishers as a freelance editor, proofreader and indexer. (pp. 75 and 143)

St Francis of Assisi (c.1182-1226) was born in Assisi in Umbria, Italy. At the age of 20, while fighting for Assisi, he was captured by the Perugians and held prisoner for more than a year. On his release, he became a soldier before returning to Assisi after dreaming about armour marked with a cross and a voice telling him to turn back. Falling out with his father, he then repudiated all his worldly goods and vowed to serve his Father in heaven. He wandered the countryside preaching the Gospel, trying to follow God's word as literally as possible.

Over time, others joined him and they called themselves the Penitents of Assisi. They went to Rome where they eventually received the blessing of Pope Innocent III and were given permission to preach repentance. Francis renamed the group the Friars Minor and they returned to Assisi where they established the Franciscan Order. Two years before his death, Francis received the stigmata, the real and painful wounds of Christ in his hands, feet and side. During the Christmas season of 1223, he decided to recreate the Nativity in a church at Greccio by installing a crib. He hoped to have a law made that people should provide for the birds and the beasts, as well as for the poor, so that all might have occasion to rejoice in the Lord. (pp. 54 and 200)

Keith Getty is a talented instrumentalist and composer who first learned to play guitar, and later the flute, attending a summer master class under the Irish flautist Sir James Galway. After several years in various aspects of the entertainment industry, Keith returned to his roots to share his faith and teach the Bible through music. He talks to church leaders and practical theologians in order that his songs reflect real issues in Christian living. Keith's website is www.gettymusic.com. (p. 10)

Hamlet is probably Shakespeare's best-known play and is universally included on the list of the world's greatest books. The longest of Shakespeare's plays, *Hamlet* is a tragedy of the 'revenge' genre. Love, justice, good, evil and madness are all played out within the dilemma of how to disentangle oneself from the temptation to mete out justice without reason. (p. 102)

Edwin Hatch (1835-89) was a devout Englishman who lived a life of spiritual simplicity. Ordained an Anglican priest in 1859, he spent some time in Toronto as Professor of Classics at Trinity College before returning to England to serve as vice-principle of Saint Mary Hall, Oxford until 1885. The first six words beginning each stanza of the hymn *Breathe on Me, Breath of*

God recall the words that Jesus spoke to his disciples when he appeared to them in the evening of the day of resurrection: *'And with that he breathed on them and said, "Receive the Holy Spirit."'* (John 20:22 NIV). (p. 129)

Frances Ridley Havergal (1836-79) was an English poet and hymn writer who began writing verse at the age of 7. She read her Bible avidly, memorising the New Testament as well as the Psalms, Isaiah, and the Minor Prophets. The hymn *Take My Life and Let It Be* was written to express her dedication. During a house visit with ten other guests, all of whom were unhappy or unconverted, Frances prayed that every one of them would come to know Jesus, saying 'Lord, give me all in this house.' She talked and prayed with each of the guests, and by the day of her departure, everyone had given their lives to Christ. Even though it was past midnight, she was so happy that she could not sleep and spent the rest of the night composing the hymn. The words 'Take my silver and my gold' expressed her intention to give all her ornaments to the church Missionary House. (p. 208)

Margaret Hayon is English by birth but has spent a great deal of her life living abroad. Much of her childhood was spent moving between England, the Gold Coast (now known as Ghana), and Nigeria. After completing a BA in African Studies at the School of Oriental and African Studies (SOAS), University of London, Margaret went to Cyprus where for five years she explored Greek villages and monasteries and converted from Anglicanism to Greek Orthodox. Returning to England, she spent several years as a civil servant before moving to Israel following her marriage to an Israeli. Since converting to Judaism, Margaret has conducted unique research into the religious traditions of the Ethiopian Jews living in Israel, photographing their manuscripts and recording their prayers and oral traditions. Teaching herself Ge'ez (the liturgical language) and a little Amharic (their spoken language), Margaret has been able to achieve a close rapport with some of their priests and elders, giving her access to material that they have refused to give to other researchers. (p. 48)

Elizabeth A. P. Head (1850-1936), an Anglican, was the wife of a London insurance broker and chairman of the Keswick Convention. She wrote a number of hymns, some of which appeared in the Keswick Hymn Book around 1937. (p. 198)

King Henry VI is a trilogy of plays written by William Shakespeare covering the turbulent Wars of the Roses between the Houses of York and Lancaster. The plays follow the available historical chronicles fairly closely, although patriotism seems responsible for some discrepancies. The French are depicted as foolish and easy to defeat, perhaps because success at the Battle of Agincourt in 1415 had created a superior attitude among the English. In addition, the French heroine Joan of Arc is portrayed as a witch and a whore. Shakespeare also wrote from a biased anti-Yorkist viewpoint for the most part, on account of the fact that the reigning monarch was descended from the Lancastrians. Part I of the play opens with the funeral of Henry VI's father and concludes with the murder of Henry VI in the Tower of London. (p. 149)

Stuart K. Hine (1899-1989) spent much of his early life in Western Ukraine where he and his wife evangelised as Christian workers and singers. On returning to Britain, Hine published many songbooks and although he retired from active ministry he continued to publish his songs, giving most of the proceeds to various missionary groups around the world. The hymn *How Great Thou Art* originated from a poem *O Store Gud* (*O Mighty God*), written in 1885 by a Swedish minister named Carl Boberg. (p. 153)

Judy Horner-Montemayor has written several hymns that are popular in modern worship. The song *Who Is Like Unto Thee* can be found in *The Songs of Fellowship Collection,* a series of albums featuring worship from both current and past songwriters. (p. 47)

Susan Howatch is an English novelist who started writing at the age of 12. After moving to the USA in her early twenties she had her first success with the publication of a short mystery, followed by a string of international bestsellers, including her family sagas *Penmarric* and

Wheels of Fortune. She returned to England where she developed a growing interest in church history through her experiences of living close to the cathedral in Salisbury. This interest set her on the road to becoming a committed Christian. Her next six novels reflected her spiritual conversion by following the lives of an assortment of Christian characters in a fictional cathedral town called Starbridge. Howatch then wrote a trilogy that involved some of the Starbridge characters 20 years on and in a different setting, at the fictitious St Benet's-by-the-Wall healing centre in London. The first book in the trilogy, *A Question of Integrity*, is a tangled love story that weaves deception, temptation, spiritual dilemmas, mental illness, depression, life crises, faith, hope and love. Howatch has successfully combined fiction with fact, by setting up the post of Starbridge Lecturer in Natural Science and Theology at Cambridge University, a post dedicated to linking the fields of science and religion. (p. 109)

Tim Hughes is a British Christian singer/songwriter who leads the worship at Holy Trinity Brompton, one of the largest

Anglican churches in London. He is also involved with Soul Survivor Christian worship events in Somerset. The song *Beautiful One* is taken from *When Silence Falls*, released in 2004. Tim's website is www.timhughesmusic.com. (p. 59)

St Ignatius of Loyola (1491-1556) was born in northern Spain. His position as page to the treasurer of Castile often took him to court where he developed extravagant tastes. In 1521 he fought for Spain and was wounded by a cannon ball, breaking a leg so badly that he was left with a permanent limp. Admiring his courage, the French soldiers allowed him to recuperate at his home, the castle of Loyola, rather than in prison.

While convalescing, Ignatius asked for some romance novels to pass the time but was given instead a copy of the life of Christ and a book on the saints. The more he read, the more he was obsessed with imitating the exploits of the saints but he was torn between daydreams of fame and glory and fantasies of winning the love of a noble lady of the court. Ignatius noticed that after reading and thinking of the saints and Christ he was at peace and satisfied, whilst his yearning for the noble lady left him feeling restless and unsatisfied. This inner conflict led not only to the beginning of his conversion, but also to a growing spiritual discernment, as described in his Spiritual Exercises. The Exercises recognise that not only the intellect but also the emotions can help us to be aware of the spirit in our lives.

Eventually Ignatius was fully converted from his old desires and dreams of romance and worldly conquests and he set out for Jerusalem, to live where Christ had died. Reaching Barcelona, he visited the Benedictine shrine of Our Lady of Montserrat where he knelt all night in vigil. Then leaving his sword and knife at the altar, he went out and gave all his finery to a poor man. His eventual visit to the Holy Land was short-lived, due to turmoil in the region and on his return Ignatius went back to Barcelona to study for the priesthood. His enthusiasm for teaching fellow students to pray attracted the attention of the Inquisition and after a stint in jail, he moved to France.

Along with six companions he decided to take vows of chastity and poverty and go to the Holy Land; while waiting in vain for a ship to take them, Ignatius was ordained a priest. Thwarted in his attempt to go to the Holy Land, he and two of his companions went to Rome instead where the Pope gave them work teaching scripture and theology and preaching. In 1539 Ignatius and his companions formed a community that would travel to wherever the Pope should wish to send them. A vow to this effect was added to the ordinary vows of poverty, chastity and obedience. Ignatius spent the next years until his death working out of two small rooms, his bedroom and his office. (p. 221)

St James (d. 62), also known as James the Just, 'brother' of Jesus, was the first Bishop or Patriarch of Jerusalem. Despite being accused by Ananias, the Jewish High Priest, of transgressing the law, he continued to preach about Jesus and, as a consequence, suffered martyrdom at the hands of an angry mob. (p. 76)

Pope John Paul II (1920-2005), born Karol Józef Wojtyla in Poland, survived Nazi atrocities, communist persecutions and an assassination attempt in his remarkable life. When Nazi occupation led to the closure of his university in 1939, he worked first in a quarry and then in a chemical factory to avoid transportation to Germany. In 1942 he began studying for the priesthood in a secret seminary of Krakow and was ordained in 1946. For the next two years he studied and ministered in Rome, France, Belgium and Holland before returning to Poland to serve as vicar in various parishes, chaplain to university students and to study further in philosophy and theology. His rise through the church was steady, being appointed Titular Bishop of Ombi in 1958, Archbishop of Krakow in 1964 and Cardinal in 1967.

He was elected Pope in 1978, being given the name John Paul II and his pontificate is one of the longest in the history of the church, lasting nearly 27 years. During this time, he established World Youth Days, bringing together millions of young people around the world. He met with numerous dignitaries, heads of states and prime ministers, encouraged dialogue between faiths, survived an assassination attempt, pushed forward a programme of canonisations and beatifications, and wrote many letters and books. More than three million people came to pay tribute to him in the days between his death and his funeral. (pp. 213 and 225)

Graham Kendrick trained as a teacher but since 1972 has been following his calling to write and sing Christian songs. He is a co-founder of *March for Jesus,* a prayer and praise event that grew from humble beginnings in the 1980s to a global phenomenon in 1994, when 12 million people from 177 nations marched through the streets to proclaim their faith in Jesus. Graham received a Dove Award in 1995 for his international work and in 2000 he received an honorary doctorate in divinity from Brunel University in recognition of his contribution to the worship life of the church. Graham's website is www.grahamkendrick.co.uk.
(pp. 31, 98 and 189)

Lisa Kimmey Bragg, along with her two sisters Andrea Kimmey Baca and Danielle Kimmey, make up the girl band *Out of Eden*. Lisa writes most of the songs, striving to share the message of God's love in a challenging society. The songs are often rooted in reality, with hope weaving through lyrics of sadness to uplift and uphold. A *'This Is Your Life Girls Event'*, promoted by *Out of Eden,* is a six-session video and music-based curriculum series aimed at young women wanting guidance with dating, modesty, acceptance, abuse, parents, and purpose in today's world. The website for *Out of Eden* is www.outofedononline.com. (p. 230)

Martin Luther King (1929-68) was born in Atlanta into a family with firm links to the African-American Baptist church. While studying theology, he became involved with Mahatma Gandhi's non-violent approach to social change. In 1954 King became pastor at Dexter Avenue Baptist Church in Montgomery, Alabama. In 1955 he was elected president of the newly-formed Montgomery Improvement Association, following the challenge to segregation on buses by Rosa Parks. This confrontation, along with further boycotts and under King's leadership, led to the Alabama laws on segregation being declared unconstitutional in December 1956.

King, now well known in America, founded the *Southern Christian Leadership Conference* (SCLC) with other southern black ministers. In the spring of 1963 he led mass demonstrations in Birmingham, Alabama, where the brutal clashes between unarmed black demonstrators and armed police made international headlines. President Kennedy responded by introducing broad civil rights legislation that eventually led to the Civil Rights Act of 1964. Mass demonstrations still continued and in August 1963 more than 250,000 protesters gathered in Washington to hear King speak. This was the platform for his now famous 'I Have a Dream' speech, from where our quote is taken. Despite being awarded the Nobel Peace Prize in 1964, his message of non-violence was overshadowed by the Nation of Islam activist Malcolm X (Malcolm subsequently left the NOI after becoming disillusioned with its leader).

The FBI director J. Edgar Hoover tried to undermine King's leadership and King's public criticism of US intervention in the Vietnam War led to strained relations with the government too. In late 1967 King initiated a *Poor People's Campaign* aimed at dealing with social problems and needs. The following year, while supporting striking sanitation workers in Memphis, he delivered his final address 'I've been to the mountaintop'. The next day, 4 April 1968, King was assassinated. (p. 232)

Paul Landers is by his own admission a Christian songwriter rather than a singer. Any regret that his voice might not appeal to the masses is replaced by his obvious enjoyment in composing songs and hearing singers bring his words to life. His song *I Kneel* is part of a collection of Christian songs in the style of folk music. (p. 105)

C. S. Lewis (1898-1963), born Clive Staples Lewis, was an Irish author and scholar. Lewis joined the British Army during World War I, arriving at the front line in France on his nineteenth birthday. In 1917, he was wounded during the Battle of Arras and sent to England to convalesce. Although he grew up in a Christian household, Lewis had been an atheist since his early teens and it was not until 1931 that he became a Christian, thanks in part to his close friendship with J. R. R. Tolkein. He became a member of the Church of England, to the slight disappointment of Tolkein, who had hoped to see his friend become a Roman Catholic. Lewis' conversion had a great impact on his writing and on his wartime radio broadcasts. His works have been translated into over 30 languages and continue to sell over a million copies a year. His best-known work is probably the *Chronicles of Narnia*, a series of fantasy novels for children incorporating Christian imagery. To date, the *Chronicles* have sold over one hundred million copies. (p. 44)

Freda Lindsay co-founded Christ for the Nations Institute, an interdenominational organisation set up in 1970 to train missionaries to minister in their own countries. The organisation provides resources for building churches, caring for orphans, supporting the nation of Israel, meeting humanitarian crises, establishing and strengthening international Bible schools and distributing Christian literature. The website for Christ For the Nations Institute is www.cfni.org. (p. 97)

Martin Luther (1483-1546) was a Christian theologian and Augustinian monk who nailed his *Ninety-Five Theses* to the door of the Wittenberg Church. The document was not just an attack on papal abuses and the sale of indulgences by church officials, but was also a defence of the Gospel. Luther believed that the Gospel taught justification by faith: Christ's own righteousness is attributed to believers, thereby ensuring their acceptance by God. Luther was the first person to translate the New Testament and then the whole Bible into German. (pp. 110 and 201)

Revd Bill McGinnis is an internet Christian minister, writer and publisher. Bill's mission is to teach the practical daily aspects of giving and receiving love, in the knowledge that love underpins a personal relationship with Jesus. His online church for Christian users is www.InternetChurchOfChrist.org. (pp. 134 and 174)

J. S. B. Monsell (1811-75) was born in Ireland and educated in Dublin. After his ordination in 1834 he worked in a series of clerical positions before moving to Guildford to work as a priest. Throughout his life he was a prolific writer and published many leaflets, sermons and papers. He also became a popular hymn writer, writing about 300 hymns, a quarter of which are still sung widely today. Tragically he died from the injuries he sustained after falling from the roof of his church during its renovation. (p. 61)

François de Salignac de la Mothe-Fénelon (1651-1715) was a French Roman Catholic theologian, poet and writer. He found himself in disgrace when as Archbishop of Cambrai he wrote works that were dismissed as religious novelties and heresy. Salignac de la Mothe-Fénelon was an advocate of Quietism, a Christian philosophy that swept through France, Italy and Spain during the seventeenth century. Quietists insist on intellectual stillness and interior passivity as essential conditions of perfection. The disgraced Salignac de la Mothe-Fénelon retreated to his diocese to administer pastoral care to his flock, throwing open his palace doors to the poor and needy. (p. 226)

Nicole C. Mullen is an American award-winning singer/songwriter and choreographer. Her involvement in outreach includes establishing a mentor group for girls called *The Baby Girls Club*, youth leadership in her local church, tutoring inner-city youngsters and participating in Across America summer camp for inner-city youth. She is also active with International Needs Network Ghana, an organisation working to free Trokosi slaves in Ghana. Nicole is the only black artist to win the Dove Award for Song of the Year, in 1998 and 2001. Her website is www.nicolecmullen.com. (p. 204)

Andrew Murray (1828-1917) was a missionary and minister in South Africa, where his gift for preaching regularly drew large crowds. He was a talented writer who produced over 240 books. Despite being plagued by ill health, Murray looked on each trial positively in his journey with God. In 1873 he helped to establish the Huguenot Seminary, a school for young women to train for educational work. When classes opened, the building was too small for all the women who had enrolled and a wing had to be added. Murray was also the first president of the Young Men's Christian Fellowship (YMCA). (p. 196)

John Newton (1725-1807), a sailor from the age of 11, was forced to enlist on a British man-of-war at the age of 18. Recaptured after desertion, he was exchanged to the crew of a slave ship en route to Africa. During this time he became immersed in a life of debauchery and immorality. It was not until Newton read the *Imitation of Christ* by Thomas à Kempis that he began to move towards conversion. After a series of miraculous rescues from death by storm, starvation, mutiny plots, and slave uprisings, Newton began to feel the sense of God's grace. After his promotion to captain of a slave ship, he started to understand the immorality of the trade and in 1754 he left the sea for good. He studied the ministry and was ordained in 1764, spending the last 43 years of his life preaching the Gospel. (p. 166)

Malcolm du Plessis, a South African worship songwriter, led worship in his local church for over 10 years. He found through his studies of Timothy and Titus that encouragement and hospitality are key gifts for leadership in the church. He recognised the close link between his relationship with God and his relationship with other people and so was able to use his gift for leading worship to encourage people in his church in their journey with God. (p. 74)

Walter Rauschenbusch (1861-1918) was born in Rochester, New York, the son of a German immigrant. After studying in Germany he returned to Rochester in 1887 to complete his studies at the theological seminary. He later moved to Berlin where he studied economics and theology at the university, before moving to England to study industrial relations. It was there that he became acquainted with the Fabian Society, a British socialist society whose aim was to transform society gradually and intellectually rather than by radical and revolutionary means.

Returning to America, Rauschenbusch became pastor of the German Baptist Church in New York City, sited in a poor and dangerous neighbourhood known locally as 'Hell's Kitchen'. His experiences there drew him to the Social Gospel movement, seeking to impact on economic and social justice by social reform. He felt the church had to be practical in its ministry and meet the needs of the weak – physically, spiritually and politically.

In 1897 he became a professor of church history at Rochester Theological Seminary. His writings include *Christianity and the Social Crisis* (1907), *Christianizing the Social*

Order (1912), *The Social Principles of Jesus* (1916), and *A Theology for the Social Gospel* (1917). He became one of the leading speakers on Christianity and social problems of his day. (p. 171)

Matt Redman co-launched the annual youth conference Soul Survivor. The event has seen a huge growth from about 2,000 people at its beginnings to 22,789 in 2005. Despite his wish to remain primarily a songwriter, and shying away from the limelight, Matt found himself leading worship to thousands of young people around the world. Feeling that God was calling out to him to plant a church within the Church of England, Matt has embarked on the exciting challenge of planting an Anglican church, The Point, in Sussex. Matt's website is www.mattredman.com. (pp. 29, 160 and 167)

William Rees (1802-83) is considered to be one of the greatest Welshmen of the nineteenth century. He grew up and worked on a farm in the north of Wales, attending school only in winter. His writing won him a prize and public recognition at the 1826 Brecon eisteddfod. Rees converted from

Methodism in 1828 when he was admitted as a member of the Independent church. His gift with words was quickly recognised and he was soon invited to preach. By 1831 he was appointed as a minister, became noted for his preaching and took up a post as minister in Liverpool. Rees wrote on a variety of subjects, encouraging people to debate politics, religion, education and slavery. (p. 175)

Noel Richards was inspired to become a Christian songwriter after listening to Graham Kendrick at a Christian concert. For the last 20 years he has been a worship leader, writing songs with his wife Tricia. Noel organised Champion of the World at London's Wembley Stadium, a huge event that attracted almost 45,000 people, making it the biggest contemporary worship event ever staged at Wembley. He was also involved with Calling All Nations, an event held in the summer of 2006 for young people and the young at heart and for worship leaders and musicians from all over the world. Noel's website is www.noelrichards.com. (p. 151)

Christina Rossetti (1830-94) grew up in London and was educated at home by her mother. The family was raised as devout Anglo-Catholics and her sister became an Anglican nun. After her brother's death in 1882 Christina withdrew from society and spent time focusing on her poetry. From a young age she had been interested in verse and her poetry was fashioned by her faith, covering subjects such as death, love, redemption and nature with her verse often reflecting her sad and melancholy character. She was courted by two gentlemen who she turned down because of faith issues; one who had turned to Roman Catholicism and the other who, after enquiring of him, was not a Christian. She never married but remained at home. She died of cancer in 1894. (p. 30)

Albert Schweitzer (1875-1965) was born in Upper Alsace, Germany, now part of France. Despite showing a talent as a concert pianist he decided to study theology in Strasbourg. On receiving his doctorate he began his ministry in the city, first as curate of the Church of St Nicholas and later as an official at the theological seminary of St Thomas. When he became aware of the urgent medical needs of Congolese Africans, he switched direction by studying medicine with a view to working as a medical missionary.

In 1913, after eight years of study and newly married, Schweitzer and his wife moved to Lambaréné in French Equatorial Africa, where he worked as a medical missionary for the Paris Missionary Society. His German nationality led to internment in France from 1917-18 and during this period he wrote two philosophical volumes about ethical thought in history. He was concerned for modern civilisation's apparent lack of will to love, suggesting that it needed a 'reverence for life'. He spent the next six years in Europe preaching in his old church, lecturing and giving concerts, taking medical courses and writing.

In 1924 he returned to Lambaréné where he rebuilt the hospital and cared for lepers, often returning to Europe to give recitals and lectures to raise money for his mission work. In 1952 he received the Nobel Peace prize, giving the $33,000 prize money and any money that came his way as a result of winning the award to fund accommodation for the lepers in Lambaréné. The hospital grew steadily, housing over 500 patients by the 1960s. Schweitzer regarded the medical mission as his home and when he died in 1965 he was buried in the mission's grounds. (p. 148)

Charles H. Spurgeon (1834-92) was the son and grandson of independent ministers. He became a Christian in 1850 at the chapel of Primitive Methodists in Colchester and after his baptism in 1851 he joined the Baptist Union. He preached his first sermon at the age of 16, became a Baptist pastor at 18 and by the age of 22 was the most popular preacher on the circuit. Spurgeon was often referred to as the 'last of the Puritans' and his misgivings about the Baptist church's growing indifference to orthodoxy led to a rift that caused him to withdraw from the Baptist Union in 1887, though he remained a Baptist until his death. (p. 96)

Jan Struther (1901-53) was the pen name of Joyce Anstruther, an upper-middle-class woman who pursued a career as a writer. She wrote poems, short pieces for several newspapers and journals and hymns commissioned by Percy Dearmer for his new collection of modern hymns, *Songs of Praise*. Even though Joyce was an agnostic, Dearmer felt that her lyrics might be more sensitively encouraging than some of the more aggressive Christian statements. (p. 217)

J. Hudson Taylor (1832-1905) learned the value of prayer while working in poverty-stricken Hull. Putting his trust in God, he became the first missionary to work in the interior of China. Challenged by storms at sea, civil war in a rebel-held Shanghai, fires and famine, Taylor prayed fervently and at the age of 22 he was dedicated in his mission work. In 1865 he founded the China Inland Mission when he opened a bank account: 'Ten pounds in the name of *The China Inland Mission*'. His initial recruitment of 24 missionaries working throughout China's interior grew to more than 800. (p. 222)

Leo Tolstoy (1828-1910) was a social reformer, pacifist, Christian anarchist, philosopher and one of Russia's most admired writers. Tolstoy's Christian beliefs were based on the Sermon on the Mount, particularly the instruction to turn the other cheek, which he saw as a justification for pacifism, non-violence and non-resistance. Despite being a wealthy member of the Russian nobility, he believed that he did not deserve his inherited wealth and he would often return to his country estate with vagrants. At the age of 82 he abandoned his family and wealth to pursue a frugal life, only to die of pneumonia a few days later. (p. 215)

Augustus Montague Toplady (1740-78) was a Wesleyan who converted to Calvinism in 1758 and became a fierce defender of their extreme views. Often rash and outspoken, Toplady's writings were considered controversial but his hymns remain an enduring legacy to the sincerity with which he lived out his faith. (p. 104)

Stuart Townend is a worship leader at Church of Christ the King in Brighton, an evangelical church of almost 1,000 members that places a strong emphasis on worship, Bible teaching, fellowship, evangelism, social action and family life. Stuart is a leading Christian songwriter whose lyrics contain a powerful mix of theology and poetry. He wrote *How Deep the Father's*

Love to reflect a sacrifice that was personal and amazing after he had been meditating on the cross. A collaborative effort between Stuart and Keith Getty resulted in one of the most inspirational Christian songs of today, *In Christ Alone*. His website is www.stuarttownend.co.uk. (pp. 10 and 24)

A. W. Tozer (1897-1963) was an American protestant pastor, preacher, author, magazine editor, Bible conference speaker, and spiritual mentor who received two honorary doctorates for his work. He became a Christian when he overheard a street preacher say, 'If you don't know how to be saved just call on God.' When he got home he climbed into the attic to call on God. In 1919 Tozer accepted an offer to pastor his first church, starting a ministry that spanned 44 years in association with the Christian and Missionary Alliance, a Protestant evangelical denomination. Writing more than 40 books, Tozer is especially remembered for his Christian classic *The Pursuit of God*. Tozer lived a simple and non-materialistic lifestyle, never even owning a car and despite his acclaim as a Christian author, he signed away much of his royalties to those who were in need. (p. 68)

Voltaire (1694-1778) was a French poet, historian, philosopher and dramatist who was passionate about fighting injustice and intolerance, especially in religious matters. Born as François-Marie Arouet, he renamed himself Arouet de Voltaire partly as a response to doubts about his parentage. His lampooning of the Duc d'Orleans landed him in the Bastille, during which time he rewrote his tragedy Oedipe. Not only did this lead to fame, it also led to a forced exile in England to escape from the enemies he gained. On his return to France, he was welcomed at the court before moving to Berlin at the invitation of Frederick the Great. Voltaire believed that the aristocracy were corrupt, that the commoners were ignorant and that the Church was only useful in providing a balance between government and people. His resolute determination to fight for human rights, including fair trials and freedom of religion, influenced the intellectual philosophies that led to the French Revolution. (p. 207)

Thomas John Watson (c.1620-86) was an English non-conformist Puritan preacher and author. He had strong Presbyterian views but his attachment to the king during the Civil War led to a brief term of imprisonment for his part in a plot to recall Charles II from exile. Ironically he was ejected from his preaching during the restoration period because of his non-conformist stance. In spite of opposition to dissenters, however, his ministry was continued privately whenever the opportunity arose. (p. 56)

Hannah Whitall Smith (1832-1911) was born in Philadelphia into a Quaker family, marrying Robert Smith in 1851. After experiencing conversions at popular 'meetings', they followed their evangelical interests, causing them to leave the Quaker movement. Robert's experiences of the Holy Spirit left Hannah with a desire for the same. After her experience in 1867 they went on speaking tours at Holiness Gatherings in America, then in England and then in Europe. Their married life was far from smooth; they had seven children, four of whom died. In the same year that her book, *The Christian's Secret of a Happy Life,* was published, their trip to Europe was cut short and they returned to America because of an incident involving Robert –

perhaps an affair. While his reputation faded, Hannah's grew. She spoke ardently about God's love for everyone and showed a deep concern for people's relationship with God. She was very outspoken for women in education and in church ministry and co-founded the Women's Temperance Union in America before working in England for the same group. (p. 183)

John G. Whittier (1807-92) was one of America's best-loved poets. His childhood on a Quaker farm in Massachusetts was ideal for observing nature and helped him to put his experiences into verse. In 1836 he became secretary of the American anti-slavery society and lived to see the successful conclusion of the abolitionist movement before he died. (p. 93)

Oscar Wilde (1854-1900) was a highly acclaimed Victorian playwright. Disregarding the fact that he was both a husband and a father, Wilde had a love affair with Lord Alfred 'Bosie' Douglas. Accused of homosexuality by Douglas' father, the Marquess of Queensberry, Wilde retaliated by suing him, only to find himself arrested, tried and found guilty of gross indecency, leading to two years hard labour. While in Reading Prison, Wilde wrote a long letter to Douglas, accusing him of selfishness and greed. The letter was published in its entirety in 1962 as *De Profundis* (Latin for 'from the depths', the first words of Psalm 130). It is a moving statement of love, sorrow and injustice, written with passion and a soul-searching journey through art from the depths of despair to acceptance and hope. Despite being an atheist, Wilde showed a deep spiritual sensitivity to Christ, probing his personality, his teachings and his life with an admiration that stemmed from his artistic outlook on life. He spent the last three years of his life staying in cheap hotels or with friends, unable to reproduce his famed creativity. (p. 126)

Bishop Thomas Wilson (1663-1755) was ordained in 1686 and was offered the Bishopric of Sodor and Man. Following his consecration, Wilson began a series of reforms in the Isle of Man, including the building of new churches, the founding of libraries and the printing of books in Manx. His book *Principles and Duties of Christianity* (1707) was the first book to be published in Manx. The judgments of his courts often brought him into conflict with the governors of the island, and in 1722 he was even imprisoned for a time. Wilson's sense of Christian duty went beyond his efforts to restore discipline; he maintained a loving devotion to the poor, setting aside a large part of his income for charity. (p. 122)

Copyright Acknowledgements

The Publishers wish to thank all those who have given their permission to reproduce copyright material in this publication.

Every effort has been made to trace the owners of copyright material and we hope that no copyright has been infringed. Pardon is sought and apology made if the contrary be the case, and a correction will be made in any reprint of this book.

Copyright permission has been granted by the following Bible publishers:

CEV

ESV

JB

KJV

From *The Authorised (King James) Version.* Rights in the Authorised Version are vested in the Crown. Reproduced by permission of the Crown's patentee, Cambridge University Press.

NEB

New English Bible © Oxford University Press and Cambridge University Press 1961, 1970.

NIRV

Scriptures taken from: *The Holy Bible, New International Reader's Version®*, NIRV®. Copyright © 1995, 1996, 1998 by International Bible Society®. Used by permission of International Bible Society. All rights reserved worldwide.

NIV

Scriptures taken from: *The Holy Bible, New International Version®*, NIV®. Copyright © 1973, 1978, 1984 by International Bible Society®. Used by permission of International Bible Society. All rights reserved worldwide.

NIV(UK)

Scriptures taken from: *The Holy Bible, New International Version Anglicised*, NIV®. Copyright © 1979, 1984 by International Bible Society®. Used by permission. All rights reserved worldwide.

NJB

©*New Jerusalem Bible* 1990 with permission from Darton, Longman and Todd Ltd.

NKJV

Scripture quotations marked 'NKJV®' are taken from the *New King James Version®*.

NLT

Scripture quotations marked NLT are taken from the *Holy Bible, New Living Translation*,

NLV

New Life Version Bible, published by Christian Literature International,

NRSV

Scripture quotations marked NRSV are taken from *The New Revised Standard Version of the Bible*,

RSV

Scripture quotations marked RSV are from the *Revised Standard Version of the Bible*,

TM

Scripture quotations from *The Message*.

TYB

Scriptures quoted from *The Youth Bible, New Century Version* (Anglicised Edition), copyright © 1993 by Nelson Word Ltd., 501 Nelson Place, PO Box 141000, Nashville, TN 37214-1000, USA.

WWE(NT)

©Worldwide English New Testament.

'Beautiful One', Tim Hughes
Copyright © 2002 Thankyou Music*
*Adm. by worshiptogether.com songs excl. UK & Europe, adm. by kingswaysongs.com tym@kingsway.co.uk

'Call on Jesus', Nicole C. Mullen
© 2001 Lil' Jas' Music/Wordspring Music LLC. Administered by CopyCare, PO Box 77, Hailsham, BN27 3EF, UK music@copycare.com

'Clothed with Splendour', Andy Bromley & Chris Donohue. Copyright © 1999 Thankyou Music*
*Adm. by worshiptogether.com songs excl. UK & Europe, adm. by kingswaysongs.com tym@kingsway.co.uk

Nick Fawcett, *Daily Prayer Time With God*
© 2003. Reproduced by permission of Kevin Mayhew Ltd, Licence Nr 705030/1

'Draw You Near', Lisa Kimmey Bragg
© Gotee Music/Rooted Deeply Music/EMI Christian Music Publishing. Adm. by Kevin Mayhew Ltd and reproduced by permission Licence Nr 705030/1

'Father, I Place into Your Hands', Jenny Hewer
Copyright © 1975 Thankyou Music*
*Adm. by worshiptogether.com songs excl. UK & Europe, adm. by kingswaysongs.com tym@kingsway.co.uk

'How Deep the Father's Love', Stuart Townend
Copyright © 1995 Thankyou Music*
*Adm. by worshiptogether.com songs excl. UK & Europe, adm. by kingswaysongs.com tym@kingsway.co.uk

'I'm Forever Grateful', Mark Altrogge
© 1986 Sovereign Grace Praise.
Administered by CopyCare, PO Box 77, Hailsham, BN27 3EF, UK music@copycare.com

'I'm on My Knees', Dave Bilbrough
Copyright © 2000 Thankyou Music*
*Adm. by worshiptogether.com songs excl. UK & Europe, adm. by kingswaysongs.com tym@kingsway.co.uk

'In Christ Alone', Stuart Townend & Keith Getty
Copyright © 2001 Thankyou Music*
*Adm. by worshiptogether.com songs excl. UK & Europe, adm. by kingswaysongs.com tym@kingsway.co.uk

'I Am a New Creation', Dave Bilbrough
Copyright © 1983 Thankyou Music*
*Adm. by worshiptogether.com songs excl. UK & Europe, adm. by kingswaysongs.com tym@kingsway.co.uk

'Lord of All Hopefulness', Jan Struther (1901-53)
From Enlarged Songs of Praise 1931.
Reproduced by permission of Oxford University Press

'O Lord, My God!', Stuart K. Hine
Copyright © 1953 The Stuart Hine Trust/Kingsway Music*
*Adm. by worshiptogether.com songs excl. UK & Europe, adm. by kingswaysongs.com tym@kingsway.co.uk

'Once Again', Matt Redman
Copyright © 1995 Thankyou Music*
*Adm. by worshiptogether.com songs excl. UK & Europe, adm. by kingswaysongs.com tym@kingsway.co.uk

'Rejoice with Trembling', Matt Redman
Copyright © 2002 Thankyou Music*
*Adm. by worshiptogether.com songs excl. UK & Europe, adm. by kingswaysongs.com tym@kingsway.co.uk

'Restore, O Lord', Graham Kendrick & Chris Rolinson. Copyright © 1981 Thankyou Music*
*Adm. by worshiptogether.com songs excl. UK & Europe, adm. by kingswaysongs.com tym@kingsway.co.uk

'River Wash over Me', Dougie Brown
Copyright © 1980 Thankyou Music*
*Adm. by worshiptogether.com songs excl. UK & Europe, adm. by kingswaysongs.com tym@kingsway.co.uk

'Tell out My Soul', Timothy Dudley-Smith
© Timothy Dudley-Smith in Europe and Africa. Reproduced by permission of Oxford University Press. All rights reserved.

'The Greatest Gift', Vicky Beeching
Copyright © 2002 Thankyou Music*
*Adm. by worshiptogether.com songs excl. UK & Europe, adm. by kingswaysongs.com tym@kingsway.co.uk

'This Is the Place', Dave Bilbrough

'Timeless Love! We Sing the Story', Timothy Dudley-Smith

'We Declare Your Majesty', Malcolm du Plessis

'We Worship at Your Feet', Graham Kendrick

'Within the Veil', Ruth Dryden

'You Laid Aside Your Majesty', Noel Richards

Bibliography

David & Pat Alexander (eds), *The Lion Handbook to the Bible* (Lion Publishing, 1975).

Peter Baelz, *Does God Answer Prayer?* (Darton, Longman and Todd, 1982).

Bishop Michael Baughen, *Getting Through to God* (Word Books, 1992).

Ian Coffey with Kim Bush, *Windows on the World from the Word*, (BRF, 2001).

J. G. Davies (ed.), *A New Dictionary of Liturgy and Worship* (SCM Press, 1986).

J. D. Douglas (ed.), *The New Bible Dictionary* (IVF, 1980).

Nick Fawcett, *Daily Prayer Time With God* (Kevin Mayhew Ltd, 2003).

Richard Foster, *Celebration of Discipline* (Hodder Christian Paperbacks, 1985).

Life's Daily Prayer Book for Women (Thomas Nelson, 2004).

Alister McGrath, *Beyond the Quiet Time* (Triangle, 1995).

B. M. Metzger & M. D. Coogan (eds), *The Oxford Companion to the Bible* (Oxford University Press, 1993).

Henry Morgan (ed.), *Approaches to Prayer* (SPCK, 1991).

Prayers from the Heart: Simple Conversations with God (Honor Books, 1999).

Alan Richardson & John Bowden (eds), *A New Dictionary of Christian Theology* (SCM Press, 1987).

Gordon S. Wakefield (ed.), *A Dictionary of Christian Spirituality* (SCM Press, 1986).

John Young, *Discipleship – Following Jesus Today* (1989).